KT-409-052

# PRIENE · MILETUS
# DIDYMA

## SUZAN BAYHAN
### Archaeologist

| | |
|---|---|
| **WRITTEN BY** | : SUZAN BAYHAN, Archaeologist |
| **TRANSLATION** | : ANITA GILLETT |
| **PHOTOS BY** | : SUZAN BAYHAN, NUSRET EREN, ENİS ÜÇBAYLAR, SELAHATTİN ERDEMGİL |
| **GRAPHIS BY** | : NURAY ÖZBAL |
| **COLOUR SEPERATION** | : RENK GRAFİK |
| **TYPE SET** | : SON SAAT GAZETECİLİK ve MATBAACILIK HİZMETLERİ A.Ş. |
| **PUBLISHED and PRINTED** | : KESKİN COLOR KARTPOSTALCILIK LTD. ŞTİ. MATBAASI |
| **DISTRIBUTED** | : KESKİN COLOR KARTPOSTALCILIK SAN. VE PAZ. A.Ş. |
| | ANKARA CAD. MUHSİRBAŞI SK. NO.6  34420 SİRKECİ - İSTANBUL |
| | TEL.: 0 (212) 514 17 47 - 514 17 48 - 514 17 49   FAX: 512 09 64 |

ISBN 975-7559-17-2

Kışla Mah. 47. Sk. 7/1  07040 ANTALYA
Tel.: 0(242) 247 15 41 - 247 16 11 Fax: 247 16 11

2008
© copyright by KESKİN COLOR A.Ş.

# INDEX

# A GENERAL OUTLINE
## OF
## IONIA

# A GENERAL OUTLINE OF IONIA

Didyma, Miletus and Priene, which were among the most important cities of ancient Ionia, are today of great value from a cultural standpoint. Ionia, cradle of various cultures in Anatolia for centuries, beginning with the pre-Archaic period, has been, with its geographical location, a centre of transition between the East and West, which has brought great economic advantages to the region.

The name of Ionia, first heard of on the coasts of West Anatolia, appears in Assyrian inscriptions as "Yavani", in Persian written documents as "Yauma" and in the Old Testament as "Yewanim".

After the fall of the Hittite Empire, Achaeans began emigrating to the coasts of West and South-West Anatolia. Around 1150 BC, with the raids of the Dorians into Greece, these migrations became more intensified, to which fact the Mycenaean ceramics found in Miletus, Iassos, Çömlekçi and Asarlık bear evidence.

The immigrants, for reasons of safety and security, generally chose to settle in coastal areas with difficult access, on peninsulas or islands.

At the end of the settlements begun with the emigration to Anatolia, the region comprising the central sector of the west coast of Anatolia, bounded by Foça to the north and the bay of Bargylia (Bodrum) to the south, and including the adjacent islands of Samos (Sisam) and Chios (Sakız), was named Ionia.

Herodotus indicates as the twelve principal cities of Ionia: Miletus, Myus, Priene in the south, Ephesus, Colophon, Teos, Lebedus in the central region Erythrae, Clazomenae, Phocaea, Samos and Chios in the north. According to ancient sources and findings, colonization in Ionia ended in the 10 th century BC. Phe fact that in many cities in Ionia the goddess Athena was worshipped, and that ceramic findings of Attic origin have been discovered there, indicate that Attica and its capital Athens, played a colonization role there which should not be understated.

Ionian cities, with their fertile lands irrigated by the Cayster and Maeander rivers, their moderate climate, their seaports which were easy to protect and open to trade, flourished in a short time. However, also for the same reasons, these cities have been the objectives of numerous assaults and migrations. To protect themselves from the latter, the cities mentioned above formed a religious and political league, the "Panionion". Excavation results have shown that izmir (Smyrna) also joined this league in the 8th century BC., therefore the Panionion must have been formed before the 8th century. The city-state notion first appears in this period.

The centre of the league was at Güzel Çamlı, on the lower parts of the northern slopes of the mountain of Samsun (Mycale). The meetings in which representatives of the member cities participated were held yearly in this sacred area, and elaborate ceremonies were arranged in dedication to the god Poseidon Helikenios. Excavations undertaken here in 1957/58 uncovered an altar cut into the rocks in the form of a theatre, which has been dated back to the 6th century BC.

Through the solidarity of this league Ionian cities showed great development both in the economic and cultural sector. This brilliant period of Ionia coincided with the second half of the 7th century BC, which is later than the foundation of the colonies (see Miletus).

As a result of the intergration of the different ethnic groups who emigrated to Ionia, with the indigenous peoples, and the ensuing mutual influencing, a very different artistic medium was created. In this, the influence of the cultures of Lycian, Carian, Lydian, Phrygian and Milesian colonies was also important.

The "Ionic Architectural Style" peculiar to this region first appeared in the 6th century

BC. based on examples from the Aiolian region.

Ionian cities which had reached their peak in all activities between the years 600 and 545 BC., were not only leaders in architecture and sculpture, but also in positive sciences and philosophy. One can see scientific thought emerge in a positive way with Thales of Miletus. The forerunners of the "Ionian Philosophy of Nature", later developed by Heraclitus of Ephesus, were also Milesian philosophers. When it was seen that mythological explanations relative to social and political subjects were adverse to facts, belief in mythological explanations of universal and natural phenomena was also shaken. Therefore, Ionian philosophers looked for an answer to the question, "Since universal phenomena are not created by the wish and will of the gods, what then is the truth at the root of these phenomena? What is the basis, the principal matter of the universe which creates itself?". They thus started this philosophical thinking in an effort to explain natural phenomena, not by religious myths, but in many cases by concrete objects and physical facts (see Miletus).

After the assaults of Kimmer in 645-626 BC, and of Lydians in 611-600 BC, Ionia fell under the rule of Persians in the year 546 BC. During this period Ionian cities were ruled by tyrants. In spite of the pressures inflicted by the tyrants, certain Ionian cities (for example Miletus) succeeded in maintaining their autonomy. The fact that Thrace, the straits, and the Marmara and Black Sea coasts were in the hands of the Persians, the commercial superiority of the Phoenicians, who were protected by the Persians, and the burden of the Persian customs taxation, all brought the Ionian cities to an economic crisis. This caused the "Ionian Revolt" headed by Miletus, to begin in 500 BC. Ionian cities in pursuit of pulting an end to tyranny attacked the Persian capital, Sardes, and completely burned and destroyed the city.

However, after this victory which was only temporary, the revolt ended when in 494 BC the Persians completely destroyed the Ionian fleet consisting of 353 ships, in the vicinity of the island of Lade. The Persians attacked Athens after this in 479 BC, but were defeated and had to retreat. The Persian fleet which had taken shelter at Mycale, was burned by the Spartans. Following this victory, the "Attica-Delos Sea League" was formed in 478 BC under the leadership of Athens with the participation of all the Ionian cities, with the objective of driving the Persians out of Anatolia.

After a dull period of about a century, spent under Persian rule, Ionia regained vitality when Alexander the Great destroyed the Persian Empire.

This region, experiencing a revival of prosperity under the Hellenistic and Roman periods, gradually began from to lose its importance from the 3rd century AD, as the alluvial mud brought by the Maeander and Cayster rivers filled the ports and, turned the environment into marshland and causing malaria to spread. The cities, reduced in size during the Byzantine period, in later times retained their autonomy from time to time under principalities and the Ottoman Empire, and made certain efforts, but they never reached their former levels.

Didyma, Miletus, and Priene lie in the south of Ionia. This region comprises the valley bounded by the mountains of Samsun (Mycale) in the north, Beşparmak (Latmos) in the south, and the bay of Latmos where the Maeander joins the sea (see Map I).

Today the bay of Latmos has become into a lake (the Bafa Lake), and the greater number of the old port cities of the region are now inland. The island of Lade, near Miletus, scene of the great sea battle, is now part of the mainland, and has the form of a hill (see Map 2).

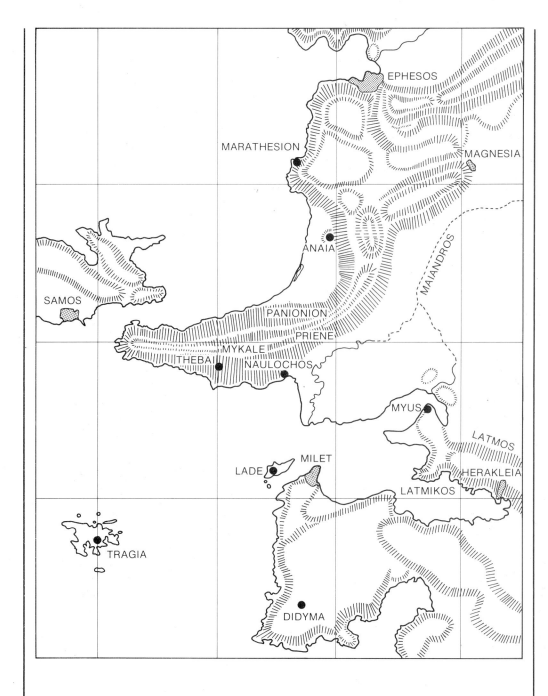

**MAP 1**    *The valley of Meander in antiquity*

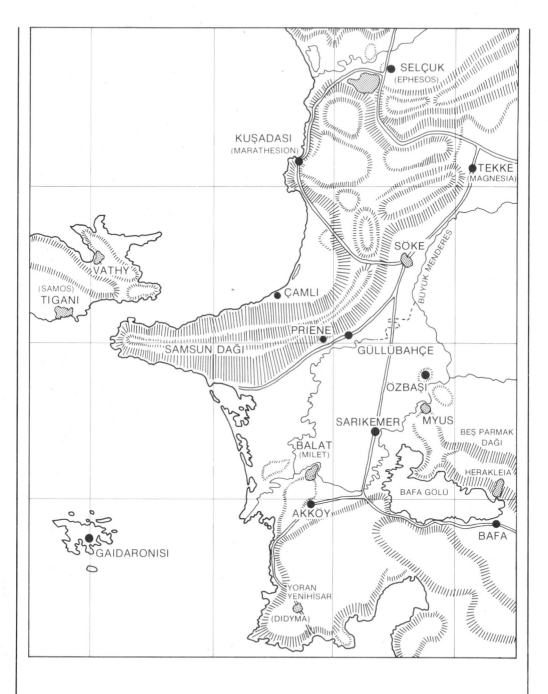

**MAP 2**   *The valley of Meander in the present day*

# PRIENE

# PRIENE

## NAME-FOUNDATION-HISTORY

It is believed that the name of Priene is not Greek but is related to pre-Greek names of Cretan origin, such as Praisos and Priansos. In recent years, the theory gains weight that Priene was one of the cities of the Kingdom of Ahhiyava, which is believed to have been founded in the Miletus region, and that its name also derives from that origin. Therefore, our knowledge of the initial foundation of the city, whose existence goes back to the 2nd millennium BC, rests on hypotheses. The fact that the location of the pre-4th century BC Priene has not yet been able to be determined up to the present day, plays an important role in this.

According to the information gathered from ancient sources, Pausanias has written that Priene was founded by Aipythos, son of Neleus of Athens, and by Philotas of Thevai, and that the native population was Carian, whereas Strabo gave the information that the city was founded by Philotas and that it was then called Kadme.

It is also believed that Priene was founded (like Pitane, Myrina, Kyme and Ephesus) by Amazon queens.

Archaeologists on the other hand, basing their claim upon the results of certain research, say that the first city was actually located at its present site, but because of the rising level of the land, o due to its filling up with alluvial deposits, it had remained inland and that during this period the outlet of the city was provided by the port of Naulochos.

One other hypothesis is that the city was situated not in the Maeander valley, but in the northern part of the mountain of Samsun (Mycale). Furthermore, it is identified with the much destroyed city of Melie situated within the ruins of the fortress visible here.

In this case, the city would have outlets via two ports, one in the north, and the other in the south (Naulochos).

The question of where? and by whom? the city of Priene, one of the oldest settlements of Ionia, was first founded, is open to debate. The information gathered from ancient sources and from recent theses differ widely. Nevertheless, to conclude, it is accepted that Priene was a small city, that it was situated on a peninsula close to Miletus and that it had two ports.

Since The site of this first city could not be determined and no concrete findings have been obtained. The only piece found is the electrum coin discovered in Clazomenae. This coin, with the head of Athena on it, and which can be dated back to 500 BC, is evidence that priene was attached to the Ionian League.

The city which, it is certain, was linked to the Panionion from its foundation onward, was, like all Ionian cities, attacked by the Kimmers in the mid-7 th century BC, but since this sack was of a transitory nature, the city recovered in a short time.

At the end of the 7th century BC, Priene was captured by the Lydians and remained for some time under the rule of this kingdom.

The 6th century BC was the most prosperous era of Priene, as for all other Ionian cities. In the beginning of this century, Bias, one of the "Seven Sages" was born in Priene, and he put into order the laws of his city. This brilliant era ended in 545 BC when Mazares, the commander of the Persian king Cyrus, attacked the city, burnt it down completely and enslaved its people. After a difficult period, Priene participated in the Ionian revolt against the Persians started in 500 BC and joined the Battle of Lade with 12 ships. However, as a result of the Persians completely destroying the Ionian fleet, the city was sacked again. The Persian fleet, defeated after its attacks on Athens, had to retreat and take refuge in the bay in front of

Mycale, whereupon the Spartans attacked and burnt the whole Persian fleet (479 BC). The "Attic-Delian Sea League" was founded immediately following upon this battle and victory, and Priene joined it in 450 BC. In 442 BC the Samos-Priene war came to an end through the mediation of this league.

Up to the mid-4th century, the city, though at times under the influence of Athens, was more under the domination of the Persians.

After the death of Mausolus (353 BC) the Persian satrapies came under the rule of Athens. According to findings and remains, the refounding of the city of Priene coincides with this period.

During the Hellenistic period, which began with the victory of Alexander the Great over the Persians and his capturing of Anatolia, all Ionian cities showed great prosperity. Alexander the Great gave the cities autonomy and abolished the excessive taxes paid to the Persians.

It is known that when Alexander besieged Miletus and the city resisted, he came to Priene and stayed there for some time (see The House of Alexander) and he made a donation to the Temple of Athena.

After the death of Alexander the Great, his commander Lysimachus (287 BC) came into power. Lysimachus acted as mediator between Samos and Priene to solve the misunder - standing about borders that had been going on for a long time. He reconciliated the two parties and gave Dryussa (north of Mycale) to Priene (283-82 BC) This misunderstanding which began with the foundation of the city was caused by the fertile land which lay to the north of Mycale, on which Samos was making continual attacks to gain posession.

During the Hellenistic period, the city came under the rule of the Ptolemaic and Seleucid Kingdoms and the Kingdom of Pergamum.

Prince Orophernes who had spent his childhood in Priene, came to rule the Kingdom of Cappadocia in 158 BC, but when he was banished from the throne a short time later, he left the state treasury to Priene for protection. His brother, King Ariarathes V of Cappadocia, asked for the treasury to be given back, but the Prieneans replied that they could only give it back to the person who had entrusted it to them and rejected the request, whereupon Ariarathes V and the King of Pergamum, Attalus II, attacked Priene together and destroyed the city completely (155 BC). Later in time, the treasury was given back to Orophernes who, in return for this kindness, made a considerable donation to the city and worked hard for its prosperity.

Treaties made in 196 and 188 BC were not able to put a stop to the fight over borders between Samos and Priene. In 135 BC, through a decree issued by the Senate of Rome, Dryussa was definitely joined to Priene and the misunderstanding was thus ended

After the death of King Attalus II of Pergamum in 133 BC, his lands were attached to Rome in conformity with his will, and Priene thus came under Roman rule.

During the Roman period, Priene went through very difficult days because of the many wars and especially the attacks of pirates, and could only achieve a more peaceful period during the reign of Emperor Augustus.

In the 1st century BC, one of the arms of the Maeander river, flowing out to the sea, provided a connection to the port, but as time went by, the alluvial mud brought down by the river caused the sea to move continually away from the city, and the connection to the port was cut off. This caused interest in the city to lessen, and Priene gradually began to be abandoned.

In the Byzantine period the city was a bishopric, and findings prove that, until the fall of the empire, it was still populated. At the end of this period Priene was completely deserted.

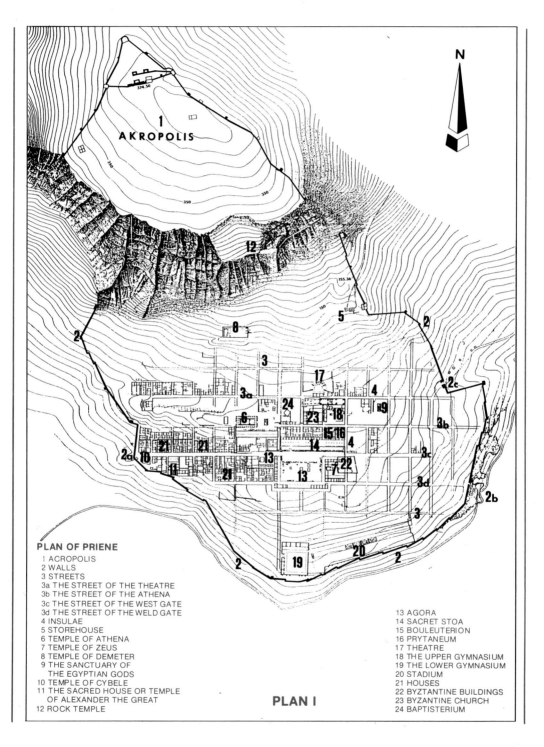

**PLAN OF PRIENE**

1 ACROPOLIS
2 WALLS
3 STREETS
3a THE STREET OF THE THEATRE
3b THE STREET OF THE ATHENA
3c THE STREET OF THE WEST GATE
3d THE STREET OF THE WELD GATE
4 INSULAE
5 STOREHOUSE
6 TEMPLE OF ATHENA
7 TEMPLE OF ZEUS
8 TEMPLE OF DEMETER
9 THE SANCTUARY OF
 THE EGYPTIAN GODS
10 TEMPLE OF CYBELE
11 THE SACRED HOUSE OR TEMPLE
 OF ALEXANDER THE GREAT
12 ROCK TEMPLE

13 AGORA
14 SACRET STOA
15 BOULEUTERION
16 PRYTANEUM
17 THEATRE
18 THE UPPER GYMNASIUM
19 THE LOWER GYMNASIUM
20 STADIUM
21 HOUSES
22 BYZANTINE BUILDINGS
23 BYZANTINE CHURCH
24 BAPTISTERIUM

**PLAN I**

# EXCAVATION AND RESEARCH WORK

The site of the remains of the city was first opened to the world of science in 1673 through a jorney of English businessmen however, research work undertaken in the 18th and 19 th centuries were more orientated to the Temple of Athena. Systematic excavation and research work only began when, in 1894 R Kekule and Karl Humann visited the city and decided to do archaeological research.

Excavation work, begun in 1895 under the supervision of Karl Humann for the Berlin Museum, was continued after his death under the supervision of Theodor Weigand. In 1898 excavation was stopped and studies to be prepared for publication were begun on the city, of which a great part was revealed.

In recent years, superficial research work is from time to time carried out in Priene by the members of the German Institute of Archaeology in Istanbul.

# 4th CENTURY PRIENE

Priene, believed to have been rebuilt in 350 BC, lies to the south west of the area of Söke, within the boundaries of Güllübahçe village, on the southern slopes of the Mycale mountain.The city was bounded on the north by the steep stretches of the Mycale,rising like a fortress, on the south by the Maeander valley, and on the south-east by the mountains of Latmos ( Beşparmak ). It was not a harbour city anymore, and its outlet to the sea was secured by the port of Naulochos ( see Map 1 ).

Strabo states the distance of this new city to the sea as being 7.5 kilometres whereas today this distance is more than 15 kilometres

Priene is a most beautiful example of ancient town planning. A factor especially important to ancient town planners was to have the whole town facing southward. This enabled the buildings to be protected from the sun in summer, but to receive more sun in winter. This implementation can be observed perfectly in Priene.

The city was built in accordance with the "grid system" developed by architect Hippo-damus of Miletus ( Plan-I ).

The 6 east-west orientated main steets were crossed at right angles by north-south orientated side streets.

*The West Gate lying on an east - west axis and the widest street of the city.*

After the excavations, from north to south, the streets named Theatre Street, Athena Street and Source Gate Street were 4.44 metres wide. However, West Gate Street, being the main street of the city, was built wider (7.36 metres).( Plan-I;3,3a,3b,3c,3d).

The side streets, generally 3.5 metres in widht were built in steps because of the sloping ground, and they largely impeded carriage transportation.

Each block (insulae), 47.20 x 35.40 metres in dimension, formed by main and side streets crossing at rigt angles, generally contained four houses.( Plan-I; 4 ).

Official and other buildings open to the public (temples, agorae, gymnasiums, bouleuterion, etc.) mostly covered the whole of a block or were continued on a second one, and were situated in the central part of the town.

The city had three gates of which one was in the west, and the two others in the east. The "East Gate" situated to the north-east of Theatre Street and which could be reached by a long, stone-paved ramp,was the main gate of Priene.

Next to the south-east gate named the "Source Gate" there was a tower with an epigraph on it, the technique of which provides proof that the tower was built at the same time as the city.

The West Gate opens onto the widest street of Priene (Plan-I; 2a, 2b, 2c).

Water for the city was provided from the sources at Mycale. It was brought down by aqueducts to the reservoirs located to the north-east of the city, and from there was distributed to the whole city by baked earthen pipes. Through this distribution many fountains (Nymphaea) were built in Priene. Some of these were situated to the south of the Athena Temple, at the eastern end of the Sacred Stoa, and in the southeastern corner of the theatre. ( Plan-I; 5 ).

*An example of the stepped side streets lying on a north - south axis In the background are the terrace walls and the propylaeum of the Temple of Athena.*

# THE CITY WALLS-THE ACROPOLIS
# (Plan-I; 1,2)

The walls surrounding Priene were 2 metres wide and 6 metres high. The front and rear faces of the walls were built of squared stone blocks while the space in between was filled up with rubble and mud. This construction technique, called "emplekton" is characteristic of the Hellenistic period. The watch towers were built in two storeys and apart from the walls. Thus, if the towers were destroyed they could be rebuilt without any harm coming to the walls. The walls between

*View of the city walls from the south - west*

the towers were usually masoned in the shape of sawteeth as in Troy.

The Acropolis, located on a very steep mass of rock in the rear part (north) of the city, was also surrounded by walls and watch towers. The connection between the Acropolis and the city walls was severed here, since there was no need for it on this steep hillside.

In the Byzantine period the walls were repaired and made more solid with some additions. During this period, the citadel in the Acropolis was given special attention and it was enlarged towards the north. The connection between the city and the Acropolis was provided by steps cut into the rocks.

Our knowledge of the Priene necropolis is extremely small, however certain findings seem to indicate that the necropolis was situated to the east of the city.

# TEMPLES

# TEMPLES

## THE ATHENA TEMPLE (Plan-I;6)

This temple, located on the culminating point of the city, rose over a wide terrace of rocks and the defence walls, and was the oldest, the most important, the largest and the most magnificent building in Priene. It was oriented on an east-west axis in conformity with the city plan and faced east. It is believed that the construction of the temple was begun at the same time as the founding of Priene (4th century BC). The architect of the building was Pythius, who also constructed the Mausoleum of Halicarnassus, counted as one of the seven wonders of the world. The temple is accepted as being a classical example of the Anatolian-Ionian architectural style.

*The Temple Athena, 4th century BC.*

The building was destroyed completely in an earthquake in ancient times and the pieces were scattered over a large area. It also suffered great destruction in a later fire. However, the construction of the plan and the reconstruction of the building have been possible through the fragments found in the excavations.

Large-grained grey-blue local marble brought from Mycale was used as construction material.

The temple, constructed in the Ionic style, consists of a pronaos, a naos (the sacred chamber where the statue of the cult was kept) and an opisthodomus. The pronaos is larger than in earlier examples. There was no opisthodomus in previous temples; it is first seen here. Pythius has taken this characteristic from the Doric style and applied it to his plan, and has thus set a model for later temples. The building, a combination of the Ionic and Doric architectural styles, emerges as a different architectural example (Form-1,2).

The plan of the temple is peripteral, with 6 columns on the short sides and 11 on the long ones. Together with the 2 columns each of the pronaos and the opisthodomus, the total number of columns adds up to 34.

The building rests on a three-stepped platform (crepis), 37.20 metres long and 19.15 metres wide. The lower diameters of the columns are one tenth of their height (a feature of the Ionic style). The columns of which the bases are built in the Ephesus type, have 24 flutes in their shaft.

The entablature resting on the capitals consists of the architrave, made up of three bands, and above it in rising order, a row of egg-and-dart moulding, dentils, another row of egg-and-dart moulding, the cornice, and on the top a cymatium decorated with plant motifs and lion-headed gargoyles. These parts were polychromed in bright colours, red and blue being the most used.

The artist, desiring to bring to the attention

*The Temple Athena, 4th century BC.*

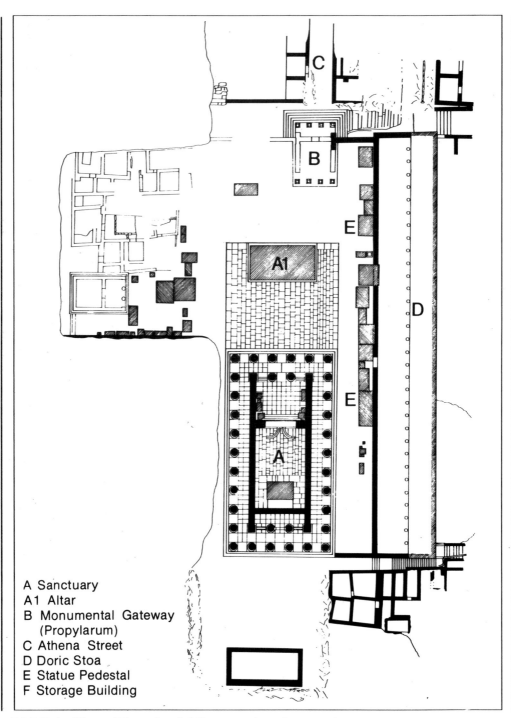

A Sanctuary
A1 Altar
B Monumental Gateway
(Propylarum)
C Athena Street
D Doric Stoa
E Statue Pedestal
F Storage Building

**FORM 1   Plan of Temple of Athena and environment**

**FORM 2**   *Temple of Athena and Altar Reconstruction*

only the architectural characteristic of his work, has put in no other decorations. There are no sculptural examples except the cult statue. Only a woman's head, revealed in the excavations, may have been one of the votive statues on display in the pronaos.

When Alexander the Great came to the region, he made a donation for the completion of the temple. This is also proven by an inscription on a tablet belonging to the temple, and now in the British Museum, which reads, "King Alexander has dedicated this temple to Athena Polias".

*The Temple of Athena, 4th century BC.*

*Rosette motifs on the entablature, the Temple of Athena.*

*Detail of entablature, the Temple of Athena.*

*Detail of entablature, the Temple of Athena.*

*The propylaeum, 1st century BC.*

However, the fact that architectural elements found on the west or rear side of the temple carry characteristics peculiar to the 2nd century BC shows that, due to various but especially to economic reasons the building could not be completed up to that period. It is understood that the temple was completed by the donation made in 158-157 BC by Prince Orophernes mentioned in the history of the foundation of the city. That the altar and the new cult statue were also erected in this period is proved by the silver coins found under the base of the statue. The cult statue of Athena was a copy of the statue of Athena Parthenos made by the famous sculptor Phidias for the Parthenon. However, it is half the size. One sees the image of the statue on coins dating from the Roman period. The standing Athena, with a helmet on her head, is seen with goatskin, spear and shield. In her right hand she holds a Nike. Fragments of the gold-plated bronze wings of Nike, and fragments of the marble left foot and arm of the goddess, indicate that the statue was 6.5 metres high. On the architraves of the temple and the altar there are inscriptions indicating that the temple was dedicated to Emperor Augustus as well as to Athena. The propylaeum, located to the east of the building, is believed to have been built during the reign of Augustus. This monumental gateway, of which the front stairs and part of the south wall are still standing, was connected to the street in front. A six-stepped flight of stairs which could be ascended on all three sides led to a porch with four Ionic columns, and from there one could reach through a single door, a large space again with four columns. According to the elements found the building had a pediment and a roof.

# THE ALTAR

The altar, siutuated to the esat of the temple was, according to findings discovered, erected in the mid-2nd century BC with the financial support of Orophernes. The altar is considered to be a model of the great Altar of Zeus at Pergamum. The building, of a horseshoe shape, was surrounded by a portico with columns, between which stood figures of women on high pedestals. The part of the building where offerings were received was approached by a flight of stairs. The reliefs decorating the altar represented scenes from the battle of the Gods and Giants. On a relief from the altar, (now in the Museum of Archaeology in İstanbul) representing the battles of the Giants, the influence of the Pergamene school of sculpture is clearly visible. In contrast with the Pergamene model, the reliefs here were placed not in the frieze but in the metopes of the lower structure. At the time of the building of the altar, the area surrounding the temple was also put into order and the front was paved with stones. Also at this time, a stoa (a porticco with a colonnade) in the Doric style was built on top of the 7 meter high terrace wall situated to the south of the temple. This stoa which was 78.40 metres long had a row of columns (32 in number) in front. In the stoa which faced the valley of Maeander, the people of the city did their daily jobs, walked and looked at the sea and the view. The rear facade of the stoa faced the temple, and therefore blocked the facade of the temple on the city side.

*Terrace walls, the Temple of Athena.*

# THE TEMPLE OF ZEUS
## (Plan-I; 7)

The temenos walls of the temple located to the east of the agora enclosed the shops in this part of the agora. This sacred precinct covered a square shaped area. There were porticoes on the north and south sides of the temenos walls surrounding the temple; there was no passage between the temenos and the agora (Form-3).

From the fragments found, one sees that the temple and altar of which today only the foundations are visible, were built in the Ionic style. The temple, of which the plan was a prostyle, was 8.50 metres wide and 13.50 metres long. In shape and style, it is a small replica of the Athena Temple, and as it has the architectural characteristics of Pythius, it is believed to have been built by him.

The temple is a simple structure, with antae created by the projecting side walls of the noas and four Ionic columns in the front. This temple which, we said above, was similar to the Athena Temple, presents

**FORM 3** *Reconstruction of the Temple of Zeus*

*Lion-headed gargoyle on the entablature of the Temple of Zeus, 3rd century BC.*

certain different characteristics. For example, the plinths of the column bases are higher and the distance between columns is greater, also the entablature is more richly decorated.

The cult statue of Zeus was housed in the naos. Based upon the fact that the noas was quite large, the theory that two statues, those of Zeus hera, were housed together here, is generally accepted.

On the east side or front of the temple are the foundations of the altar, a structure with the dimensions of 4.76 x 3.57 metres.

It is believed that the temple, the construction of which, it is understood, was begun in 330 BC, was finished in time for the yearly festival of presentation of votive offerings in honour of Zeus Soter and Athena Nike (the beginning of the 3rd century BC).

Within the temenos area, to the north-east there are the remains of the Byzantine fortress and the church attached to it.

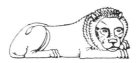

# THE TEMPLE OF DEMETER

## (Plan-I; 8)

This temple dedicated to Demeter, the goddess of fertility - earth, and her daughter Kore, was built the founding of the city, on the terrace situated just below the steep slopes of the Acropolis, at a height of 129 metres. From the sea. The building, covering an area 45.05 metres long and 17.75 metres wide, of Temenos lies on an east-west axis, with the entrance on the east side.

This temple differs from the peripteral temple type and displays a different from. A rectangular protective wall surrounded the building; in front of the entrance door stood two statues of priestesses. According to the inscriptions on their bases, one of the statues, a bronze one, represented the priestess Timonossa, and the other, a marble statue of the priestess Nikesso, revealed in the excavations and today on display in the Pergamum Museum in Berlin, is of great importance from the viewpoint of the History of Art, although it lack the head and the right arm. It is understood that these two priestesses were the head priestesses of Demeter and Kore.

To the south of the entrance, there is a group of simple houses where temple personnel and priestesses lived. On the north side of the entrance one sees a square-shaped building, and a little beyond this building which is believed to be a water tank there is an altar, believed to have been built at a later period.

After crossing the big courtyard where processions and festivals were held, one reaches the temple, at the west end of the temenos. The distance between the temenos and the walls of the temple is quite short. In the front part of the temple there is an

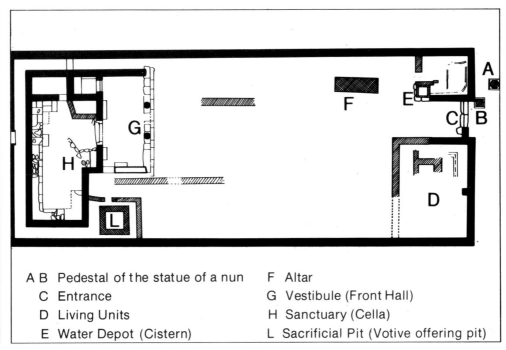

| A B | Pedestal of the statue of a nun | F | Altar |
| --- | --- | --- | --- |
| C | Entrance | G | Vestibule (Front Hall) |
| D | Living Units | H | Sanctuary (Cella) |
| E | Water Depot (Cistern) | L | Sacrificial Pit (Votive offering pit) |

**FORM 4. Plan of the Temple of Demeter**

entrance-hall (vestibule) with two Doric columns and a stone-paved floor. From here one goes on to the Cella (the sacred room). The south side of the cella is narrower, and on the north side there are two little rooms. Apodium was build along the west wall of the cella, for half the length of the side walls. Votive steles were displayed on this podium. Just in front of the podium two altar stones can be seen in situ. Outside the temple, between the narrower south side of the cella and the vestibule there is a square-shaped sacrifical hole (Form-4). Blood from the animals offered to the goods was gathered here and used for sanctification. A great number of grotesque figurines have been found around this hole. The Demeter figurine found among the votive offerings was represented with a corn sheaf, (her attribute) in her hand. This figure can also be seen on early Prienean coins. Most of the figurines were made in the 3rd and 4th centuries BC. One of the statue bases of the entrance, according to the inscription on it, dates from the 2nd century BC, whereas the altar displays characteristics of the Roman period. To judge from these, one can see that the temple had maintained its importance for several centuries.

# THE SANCTUARY OF THE EGYPTIAN GODS

## (Plan-I; 9)

This sanctuary situated on the terrace south of the theatre, on the block (insula) formed by the theatre on the north, the Athena Street on the south and the side streets at right angles to these on the east and west, covers an area 47 metres long and 31 metres wide. As the land sloped, the south end was supported by a 5 metre high terrace wall which displayed excellent stone workmanship. The building, as in the Egyptian examples, is a temple open to the sky. The remains of a 14.60 metre long, 7.31 metres wide and 1.73 metre high altar which served as a temple have been found in this area. Stairs, understood from the marble blocks on the south side of the temple to have been 5 metres wide and 7-stepped, led to the place where votive offerings were presented. The square-shaped propylaeum to the north-west of the sanctuary and the gallery along its western wall were built at a later period. That the sanctuary was dedicated to Egyptian gods is understood from the epigraphs found there. In an epigraph found within the temenos area the names of such Egyptian gods as Isis,Serapis, Osiris, Anubis and Harpocrates are mentioned, and in the inscriptions on the wall of the propylaeum, besides detailed information on the cult, it is also stated that the rites should be conducted by an Egyptian priest, or if not, then by Isis. In the event of the violation of these rules, the punishment is defined as being 100 drachmae. From the very severe punishment and from the inscriptions which explain in full detail the cult of the Egyptian gods, one can see that the Prienean people were not familiar with this tradition.

We can explain the coming of the Egyptian cult to Priene in two ways. The cult of the Egyptian gods gained importance in this region either when, following the Laodicean War (246-241 BC), King Ptolemy III of Egypt tried to bring the Aegean region under Egyption rule, or when Priene which had commercial relations with Egypt, wanted to please Egyptian businessmen by dedicating this sanctuary to Egyptian gods.

The stone workmanship of the altar and the writing techique of the epigraphs in the area show that the building was erected in the 3rd century BC.

# THE TEMPLE OF CYBELE
## (Plan-I; 10)

Two houses to the west of the city where Prienean houses were densely clustered, acquired a sacred identity according to the findings. One of these is accepted as the Cybele Temple, and the other as the sacred house or Temple of Alexander. The first building, situated on the block south-east of the West Gate and south of the street leading to the West Gate, was dedicated to the Mother Goddess Cybele. The temple consists of a courtyard surrounded by simple, modest walls of pentagonal shape and a sacrifical hole in the centre. The statue of Cybele (marble), revealed in the excavations, also indicates that this place was dedicated to the goddess Cybele. Generally the poor used to worship the Mother Goddess Cybele. The simplicity of the building and the findigs indicate that the cult of goddesses was not supported by the state.

# THE SACRED HOUSE OR TEMPLE OF ALEXANDER THE GREAT

## (Plan-I; 11)

This house, situated to the east of the Cybele Temple, is also accepted, according to the findings, as a sacred building, a temple. It is known that Alexander the Great lived in this house during his siege of Miletus in 334 BC and made large donations for the construction of the Athena Temple during his stay in Priene. The people of the city, in order to express their gratitude to him, must have dedicated this house to his memory and built it into a place where people could worship him.

An inscription on the Sacred Stoa states that in Priene there was a sacred place dedicated to Alexander the Great and that donations amonunting to a total of 1000 drachmae were made in the year 130 BC by the important persons of the city for its repair.

The plan of the building, apart from repairs and certain additions, is not different from a normal house plan. The entrance door, on the west, opens onto a side street. The house consists of a big courtyard, a large there-columned room and various other rooms. The remains of a podium on which votive articles were displayed can be seen in the large room. In one of the small rooms a sacrificial table stands. Excavations made here revealed marble statuettes, terra cotta figurines and the upper part of the statue of Alexander (marble). The characteristics of the Hellenistic period are clearly visible in the statue which was taken to the museum in Berlin.

One understands from an incsription on this building (also in the museum in Berlin) that a condition was laid down allowing only persons dressed in white to enter the temple.

# THE ROCK TEMPLE

## (Plan-I; 12)

Stairs cut into the rocks on the steep southern slopes of the Acropolis provided the link between the Acropolis and the city. The rocky area just above these steep stairs was flattened to make a platform 5 metres wide and 12 metres long. To the east of the stairs a Hermes figure carved in low-relief, and beds hollowed out of the rock to serve as bases for statues can be seen. On the west side of the stairs there are alcoves for the display of votive articles.

*The Agora, a general view of the Temple of Zeus.*

# THE AGORA
# (Plan-I; 13)

Agoras had an important place in the daily life of ancient cities. Here were held meetings to discuss various subjects, and festivities were also arranged here.

The Priene Agora which was defined by Pausanias as being "a characteristic example of Ionic agoras", cannot be the agora of which we see the remains today, since the remains include Doric elements.

The agora, built in the 3rd century BC, covers two blocks (inculae) in the central part of the city and is 75.63 metres long and 35.40 metres wide. Parts of the street on the south side of the agora and of the side street running through the central part and crossing it perpendicularly, remain within the agora area. The north side is bounded by the West Gate Street which is the main street of the city. The agora, of a horseshoe shape, has one side open, and is surrounded on the other there sides by stoae (Form-5). These stoae which have, apart from the corner columns, 18 columns each on the east and west sides, and 30 columns on the south side, are constructed in the Doric style. At the rear parts of the south and west side stoae are a row of rooms (shops). The shops at the rear part of the east stoa remain in the temenos area of the Zeus Temple. Some of the rooms in the middle part of the south side were remaved and this space was turned into a large hall by enclosing it with walls half the height of the columns on the north side. In the middle of the hall stands a row of columns. As the site is sloped, the south side of the agora was supported by a substructure. In the middle of this side is a door with twin

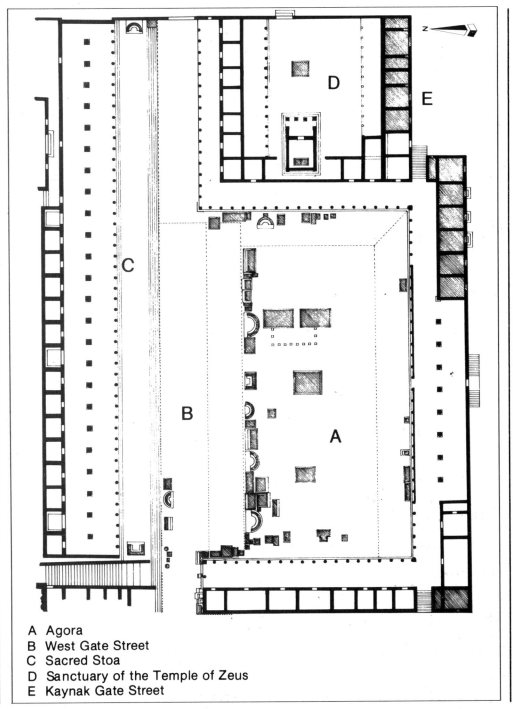

A  Agora
B  West Gate Street
C  Sacred Stoa
D  Sanctuary of the Temple of Zeus
E  Kaynak Gate Street

**FORM 5 Plan of Agora and environment**

**FORM 6** *Northwest corner view of Agora (Reconstruction)*

flights of stairs in front which opens onto the street in front. Besides this door, the agora has two more entrances. These are two doors with stairs, situated one at the south-east and the other at the south-west.

Statues representing the notabilities of the city stood, most of them in the northern part, others in the front of the stoae. These statues in marble and bronze were polychromed in bright colours, and created a very impressive atmosphere. In this area which in ancient times had the aspect of an art gallery, today only the bases of the statues are standing. (Form-6) These pedestals, some of which area quadrangular and others semi-circular, also served as benches for people to sit on.

In the middle of the agora stood an altar 6.20 metres long and 5.15 metres wide, dedicated to the god Hermes. On the east side of the altar of which only the foundations are visible, there are two separate platforms. These were believed to be boxes built for the

**FORM 7** *General view of southwest side of the Sacred Stoa*

prominent persons of the city. The 12 bases on their front side were built to support the wooden poles which carried the awning. To the left of the agora and adjacent to it is a small agora, a market place where various food, clothing, and other articles were sold. Excavations revealed stone tables (counters) here on which the items for sale were displayed.

# THE SACRET STOA
## (Plan-I; 14)

This 12 metre wide and 116 metre long building, situated to the north of the agora and West Gate Street, was constructed in the period where, beginning with the mid-2nd century BC, large and imposing buildings were the fashion. A fragment of a inscription on the architrave of the building also bears evidence that the Sacret Stoa was erected (130-112 BC) with the donation of King Ariarathes of Cappadocia.

It has been established that the building situated 1.5 metres higher than the agora, was erected over a 3rd century BC altar, (the existence of which was proven by the findings) by enlarging and developing it.

A 6-stepped stairway in the front opening onto the street leads to wide gallery open to the sky. This gallery has a marble-paved floor and is 6.47 metres wide. This was the promenade area of the stoa. At the east and west ends of the gallery were benches of which one was in an exedra and the other in a horseshoe shape (Form-7). The inscriptions on the backs of the seats mention certain names from among the people of Priene. A 3-stepped stairway at the rear of the promenade area leads to the gallery, separated into two parts by columns. 49 Doric columns in the front row and 24 Ionic ones in the rear row stood along the length of the building and supported the roof. The Ionic columns in the second row were higher than the Doric columns in front, and they had no fluting in the lower part of the shaft. The roof was wooden, and that the short sides had pediments could be understood from the elements found. At the rear there are 15 rooms. Three of these rooms, the stone workmanship of which is excellent, are of exedra design. It is understood that the 9th room from the west was consecrated to the cult of Roman gods and to Emperor Augustus. The inscriptions and drawings on the walls of this room make it clear to us that the Julian (Roman) calendar was begun to be used in West Anatolia in the year 9 BC.

It is believed that these rooms were used for the conservation of the State and the Athena Temple archives.

There are many inscriptions on the walls of the stoa. These inscriptions, which only on the west side number 1400 lines, generally give very detailed information on the city life. We can get an outline of city life at that time from these inscriptions.

*The Bouleuterion, 2nd century BC.*

# THE BOULEUTERION
## (Council House)

## Plan-I; 15)

Political life in Priene consisted, as in other Ionian cities, of a two assembly system. One of these was the "Boule", an advisory council with a lesser number of members, called the Bouleutus, this was the "Demos", an assembly of citizens, which was made up of all the people of Priene and which held its meetings in the Ecclesiasterion or in the theatre.

The Bouleuterion is the best preserved building in Priene. Although at first it was thought to be the Ecclesiasterion, later, since it could only seat 640 persons, it was accepted as the Bouleuterion. The Boule held its meetings here and took the decisions relating to the administration of the city. The assembly of citizens on the other hand, meet once a year and elected the administrators.

The building, situated just behind the Sacred Stoa, is bounded on the north by the Athena Street and is 20 metres wide and 21 metres long. The edifice is surrounded on three sides by rows of benches (Auditorium) and has 16 steps on the north side and 10 each on the east and west sides. The seats were reached by the stairs on the east and west.

In the exact centre of the building is a marble altar (Form-8,9). The altar, understood to have been built in the 2nd century BC, is decorated with wreaths tied with bulls' heads, and above these are reliefs ornamented with busts of gods.

The Bouleuterion has two main doors in the front (south). There is a niche between these doors. The niche is believed to have

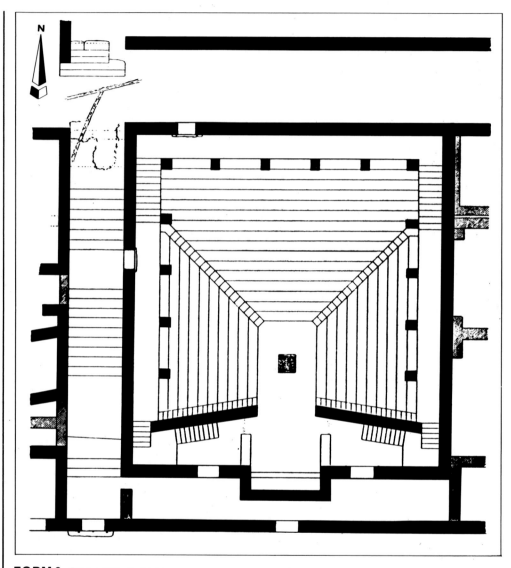

**FORM 8** *Plan of Bouleuterion*

been used as desk. The benches in front were added later.

The building has two more doors on the north and west. People seated in the upper rows could go out into the side street and the Athena Street through these doors. These secondary doors also enabled latecomers to enter the hall silently.

There is no evidence to show that the building had windows. It is assumed that the lighting was provided by the south side which was open to the sky. The building was covered by a wooden roof which was supported by the walls, and the supporting columns standing on the tompmost step of the rows of seats. One can see from the

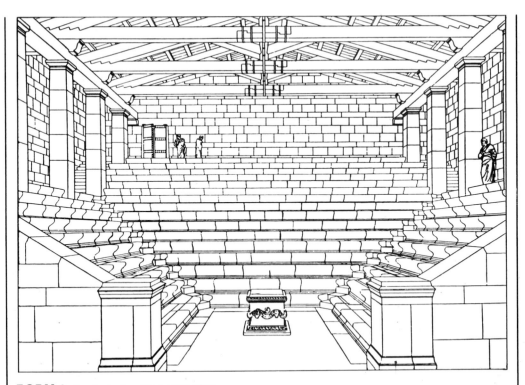

**FORM 9** *Bouleuterion Reconstruction*

*The Bouleuterion, 2nd century BC.*

*The Bouleuterion, 2nd century BC.*

remains that, to enable the roof which was quite wide to be easily supported, the supporting columns were moved inside by 2 metres and their lower parts were fortified by certain additions.

It is a debatable question whether the building was constructed at the same period as the altar or at an earlier period. The fact that all the architectural characteristics of the Bouleuterion are visible on the Sacred Stoa is evidence that it was built before the other one. We can thus assume that the building was erected in the same period as the altar ( 150 BC).

# THE PRYTANEUM

## (Plan-I; 16)

To the east of the Bouleuterion and adjacent to it is the Prytaneum, also built in the 2nd

century BC, however, because of the modifications made in the Roman period, it is difficult to see remains dating from the earlier period.

The Prytaneum is the building where daily administrative operations were executed, where the members of the Advisory Coucil (the Boule) met, and where visitors of the State were entertained.

However, the utmost function of the building was to ensure that the fire in the "Sacred Hearth of the City" situated here and dedicated to the goddes Hestia and all the other hearths of cities burned perpetually. This task, considered sacred from a religious point of view, was also paid the expenses.

The entrance door of the Prytaneum is in the middle part of the south side. In the room to the east of the entrance stands the Sacret Heart in which the sacred fire burned. The 30 centimeter high heart, made up with rubble, is believed to date from earlier periods.

*The Prytanéum, 2nd century BC.*

*Insription found in the Prytaneum.*

*The Theatre 4th century BC.*

# THE THEATRE
## (Plan-I; 17)

The theatre, built in the 4th century BC in the northern part of the city, making good use of the sloping land, has reached the present day in a well-preserved condition. Although having undergone many changes afterwards, it has not lost its Hellenistic characteristics. Like all ancient Greek theatres, the building consists of three main parts: the Skene (the stage building), the Orchestra (the horseshoe shaped space in the middle), and the Cavea (the space where the spectators sat).

The evolution of ancient cultures can be observed step by step in the Priene theatre by following, starting with its first construction, the changes and additions later made to it.

Particularly the well-preserved state of the skene which showed great development, makes this observation much eaiser. From this point of view the Priene theatre is as important in the present day as it was in ancient times.

We understand that the theatre was built at the same time as the founding of the city, because in a inscription of honour dedicated to Apellis in the years 332-330 BC just after the founding of the city there is mention of the theatre. As Greek drama in its origins went back to Dionysus, the god of wine, a general ceremony was held in front of the altar to Dionysus before the performances, usually with the offering of a sacrifice to the god. After this ceremony the performance began, and the chorus in attendance on two sides of the orchestra began a dialogue. In this period, the theatre had the function of a sacred area, where votive offering ceremonies and celebrations dedicated to the god Dionysus were held.

This first theatre consisted of the cavea, the orchestra and the prohedria (front row of seats). The setting for the performances was the orchestra, therefore the most coveted place in the theatre was the area surrounding it. In the middle of the prohedria, as in all ancient theatres, stood an altar dedicated to the god Dionysus. And here were also the seats for the nobility. The number of actors increased as the performances, at first in the form of purely ritual celebrations, grew in time into dialogues of religious content, and still later were dramatised and began to be performed by actors. The stage building required for this was built in the rear part of the orchestra.

In the beginning of the 2nd century BC a proskene was added to the front part of the skene. Towards the middle of the same century, the inadequacy of the orchestra which functioned as the stage, and the wish to perform the plays on a high platform, led to changes being made in the stage building and the proskene, from which a model of the present day theatre stages evolved. The facade of the stage, facing the theatre, was richly decorated with painted wooden plates termed pinaks.

Taking into consideration all the present day remains, it has been calculated that the cevea of the horseshoe shaped theatre had 50 rows of seats and that it had the capacity to seat an audience of 5,000 persons. To facilitate the entrance and exit of the spectators 6 stairs were cut into the rocks. The rows of seats were covered with marble. The upper parts of the rows were destroyed while the lower parts are extant. Square-shaped little holes visible in these rows of seats were made to hold the posts of the awnings used for protection from sun and rain.

In the middle part of the 5th row of the cavea stands a second prohedria. These seats, which had lions' paw profiles, were made for distinguished persons. When, as mentioned above, in the mid-2nd century plays began to be performed on the proskene, the front prohedria lost its importance. It became imperative to construct this second prohedria to enable a better view of performances. Also at this time two small doors were built on each side of the altar.

The orchestra has a floor of pressed earth is encircled by the prohedria consisting of five armchairs with seats and backs. The armchairs were placed with differing distances between them. In the exact middle of this row of seats there are the remains of an altar dedicated to the god Dionysus. It is understood from the inscriptions on the altar that it was built in the beginning of the 2nd century BC with the donation of a certain Pythotimos. In a inscription in front of the row of armchairs the name Nysios is mentioned. The inscription shows a different character, but it is accepted that the armchairs were also built at the same time as the altar.

At the rear part of the prohedria, on the passage leading to the rows of seats, there is a 1.85 meter wide space with a stone-paved floor. This must have been built both to facilitate spectators reaching their seats and to canalize rain water. At the east end of this passage stands a circular pedestal belonging to a bronze statue, and at the west end the base of a water clock.

The sides of the theatre are supported by walls displaying excellent stone workmanship. At the lower ends of these walls where they join the orchestra there are square-shaped bases. On these bases once bronze statues stood. It has been understood from the inscriptions on these that the statues were made by the sculptor Cleandrus, who had gained the title of Stephanephorus, and they were dedicated to the god Zeus and the people of Priene.

The stage section consists of the rectangular skene, with a door opening onto the street in front (the Theatre Street), and the proskene

*Example of armchairs in the Probedria.*

*Statue base with inscription, 2nd century BC.*

**FORM 10** *Reconstruction of Theatre Building*

situated in front of this. This two-storeyed stage building is 18.41 metres long and 5.82 metres wide. Each floor has three rooms.

The doors of the lower floor rooms open onto the proskene. The stage building which underwent big changes in the Roman period (2nd century AD), was rebuilt by pulling down the upper storey front walls completely and moving them 2 metres back. Thus the proskene, namely, the performance area, was enlarged. Here also were three doors which gave onto the proskene. It is very easy to discern between the Hellenistic and Roman stage buildings by studying the construction techniques.

The very well-preserved proskene is 21 metres long, 2.74 metres wide and 2.70 metres high. Fragments of architrave and cornice, belonging to the building which had 12 columns in the Doric order in front, were also found in a well-preserved state. On the inner and front rows of columns of the proskene lie tie-beams. In the intervals of this row of colomns are three doors for the entrance end exit of the actors. The intervals between the other colomns were closed with painted wooden plates. These could be changed when desired (Form-10).

One can see from the traces on the fragments found that the columns and other elements were polychromed in various colours.

There are two circular statue bases in the front part of the proskene. On one of these once stood the statue of Apollodorus and on the other that of Thrasybulus. In the agora too there were statues of these persons who had an important place in the history of Priene. It is understood from the inscriptions on their bases that the statue of Apollodorus was made on the wish of the city council of Priene and that of Thrasybulus on the wish of his wife, both in the year 130 BC. It is accepted that the proskene was also built at this time.

Between the setcion where the audience sat and the stage building, were two side entrances termed parados. It has been established from the remains that the paradoses situated on the east and west were closed with iron fences in the Roman period.

# THE GYMNASIUMS

There were two gymnasiums in Priene. One of these was the 'Upper Gymnasium" located in the central part of the city, and the other the "Lower Gymnasium" on the south which was joined with the stadium.

In these buildings which we can compare to present day elementary and secondary educational institutions, children and young people, besides receiving education, were also trained in physical exercises by the practice of various sports.

The upper gymnasium was reserved for boys (paides) and youths (ephebes), and the lower gymnasium for young men (neoi).

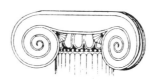

*General view of the Ephebeion, the Lower Gymnasium, 2nd century BC.*

*Examples of inscriptions written by the pupils on the wall of the Ephebeion.*

*Examples of inscriptions written by the pupils on the walls of the Ephebeion.*

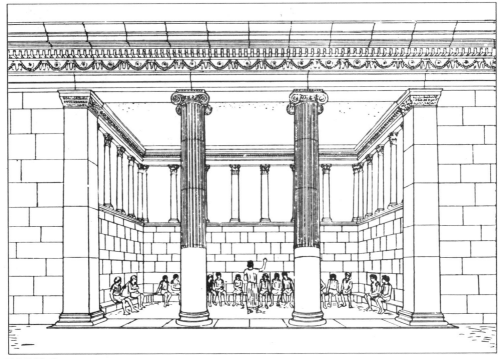

**FORM G** *Lower Gymnasium - Ephebeion Reconstruction*

# THE UPPER GYMNASIUM (Plan-I; 18)

This building, of which it is difficult to establish the initial plan because of the big changes it underwent during the Roman and Byzantine periods, was situated between the theatre and the bouleuterion with the Theatre Street on its north the Athena Street on its south.

The building, which is understood to have been built at the same time as the founding of the city (4th century BC), consisted of rooms encircling a courtyard with a peristyle. From this period only the outer walls on the south and east, the remains of the entrance door (the propylaeum) on the east, and the foundations of the exedra (altar) in tne courtyard are visible.

The remains of the naiscos (small temple) are situated in the north-west corner of the courtyard and belonged to the cult of the Roman Emperors. To the east of the temple lies the pool dated back to the Byzantine period.

During the Roman period baths were built on the south side of the gymnasium, thus increasing the facilities.

The gymnasium covered one insulae. Whether it also included the insulae in front is uncertin since the excavations are not completed.

# THE LOWER GYMNASIUM

## (Plan-I; 19)

This building constituting a complex with the stadium to the south of the city, is well-preserved. The square-shaped Palaestra (sports ground) is surrounded by galleries with Doric columns (porticoes). On the north and west sides of the palaestra, which is 34.35 metres wide and 35.15 metres long, there are rooms. A second row of columns was added to the northern gallery, thus enabling more light to enter the rooms. In front of the largest room, situated in the middle of the north side, stand 4 Ionic columns, and inside there are rows of seats along the walls.

According to Vitruvius, this hall was the Ephebeion where classes were held for the pupils. Many inscriptions written by the pupils in their handwriting and containing their own or their fathers names, and of which examples can be seen on the walls, are also evidence that this section was a classroom. (Form- G ).

On the walls of the washrooms, situated in the north-west corner, the wash-basins nad water channels can still be seen. The other rooms were reserved for practising in various branches of sport.

The gymnasium has two doors, one in the east and the other in the west. In the front of the west entrance stand two columns in the Doric order. This door, of the appearance of a propylaeum, opens onto the stepped side street. The door on the east is connected to the stadium.

Inscriptions found give evidence that the lower gymnasium was built in the year 130 BC together with the stadium.

*Starting point bases of the stadium.*

*Detail of lion-beaded gargoyle on the entablature of the stoa.*

# THE STADIUM

## (Plan-I; 20)

The structure lying parallel to the walls to the south of the city, is adjacent to the east side of the palaestra of the lower gymnasium and is connected to the door of the palaestra.

Thus they have the appearance of a complex structure. As the site was sloped, the section allocated to spectators was only built on the north side of the stadium. To the rear of the seats is a stoa in the Doric style, facing south. The stoa was used for practising before the games. The front part of the 190 meter long and 6 meter wide building was allocated as a promenade area and was open to the sky. In front of the promenade area lie rows of seats

*Middle section of the tiers of seats in stadium, 2nd century BC.*

*Elements of entablature of the stoa in the stadium, general view.*

in steps. The top of a section in the exact middle of the steps on which the spectators sat was covered with marble. The stoa, the promenade area and the rows of seats, were all reached by stairs on the west side.

In front of the rows of seats lies the 191 meter long and 20 meter wide racecourse where the games were held. On the west side of this area, one can see two rows of bases with hollow middles, of which 8 are in the front row and 10 in the rear one. The bases in the front row were used in the Hellenistic period as the starting points for the races. Those in the rear row are the bases of a more grandiose exit gate, built in the Roman period. At the east end of the racecourse there must have been a column marking the finishing point of the races, but no trace of it has been found. The stadium, according to the inscriptions on it, was built in 130 BC.

# HOUSES

# (Plan-I; 21)

Priene houses, most of which have been revealed in the excavations, present a very simple form of building, but although they have been used for centuries, they are of great value from the point of view of civil architecture, since they convey daily life as it was from the Hellenistic period up until the present day. The entrances of the houses usualy gave onto narrow side streets. Entrance to the houses with doors on the main street was provided by long and narrow corridors. Walls built with rubble and mud have carefully squared stone blocks on their street sides. There are generally no windows

*West ate Street and the houses on the stepped side street.*

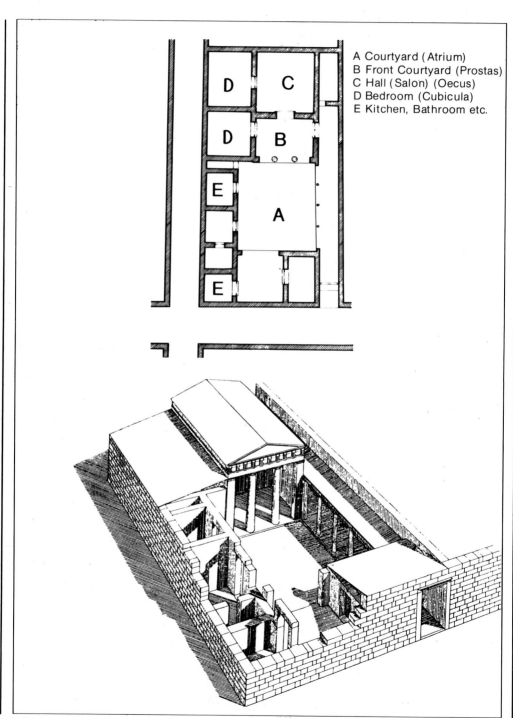

A Courtyard (Atrium)
B Front Courtyard (Prostas)
C Hall (Salon) (Oecus)
D Bedroom (Cubicula)
E Kitchen, Bathroom etc.

**FORM 11 Plan and reconstruction of Priene type house**

or doors on the street side. If windows were built at all in the outer facade, they were built high up, thus preventing the inside of the house beeing seen from outside. 79 centimeter long and 52 centimeter wide terra-cotta plates with holes, found in the excavations, are believed to be window grids.

In the central part of the houses was a courtyard (atrium), onto which doors and windows of rooms of different dimensions opened. Light and air circulation was provided from here. The Largest room of the house, namely, the drawing-room (Oecus), always faced the south, and its front part was separated from courtyard by an entrance hall (Prostas), sometimes with columns and sometimes without.

Next to the drawing-room were generally two bedrooms (Cubicula) of smaller dimensions. In the courtyard were divisions which changed in number according to needs and which constituted the other elements of the house such as the kitchen, bath, etc. The height of the rooms were, as in Mediterranean architecture, 5.5-6 metres. The house interiors were of quite simple appearance. Walls were in general plastered and whitewashed. The lover parts of some walls were given the appearance of marble by plastaring with stucco. Here there were no polychromed mosaics and frescoes, of which one sees beautiful examples in the houses in Ephesus and Pompei. Floors were made of pressed clayey earth. The doors had marble thresholds and were two-leaved. From the traces of stairs seen in the lower floors of some houses, one understands that there were also two-storeyed houses in Priene. The houses were covered with tile roofs (Form-11).

Numerous house articles such as fragments of bronze bedsteads, marble tables, hearths, bronze and iron untensils, terra-cotta pottery, oil lamps, statuettes and coins have been found in excavations. A bathtub of normal measurement found in the bathroom of one of these houses is remarkable. Most of the artifacts are dated back to the 4th century BC. The structure of these houses differ from peristyle house-type,and their origins are believed to go back to Mycenaean houses. More recently, they are considered to have been a developed form of the megaron houses.

Part of the houses built in the 4th century BC have in later periods been turned into peristyle houses by the application of certain alterations. We can indicate as an example to this, the house occupying the block on the north-western corner of the Athena Temple on the Theatre Street (Form-12). This building, restored in part after the excavations, is the largest and the best preserverd house in Priene. To judge from the workmanship of the masonry of the facede on the street side and from the valuable findings discovered in the house, it must have belonged to an important person.The altar dedicated to Zeus Olympus, found in the house, is also evidence of this, and shows that the first owner was a Stephanephorus. A person receiving this title conducted for one year all religious ceremonies and celebrations, and the year was named after him. Therefore, it was a great honour to receive this title,. But to be a stephanephorus one had to be very wealthy, because all the expenses of the ceremonies and festivities were paid by this person.

The entrance door of the house which had a total of 26 rooms, is situated in the middle of the facede and opens onto the street. From a small square courtyard at the entrance one goes on through another door into a second courtyard. The first door on the right opens into the servants room, the second door into the rooms for gentlemen and the door across into the rooms for ladies. On the gentlemens side, a central courtyard is surrounded on all sides by rooms of differing sizes, and thus creates a peristyle house. The ladies side is similarly arranged and columns have been added to the courtyard. On careful examina-

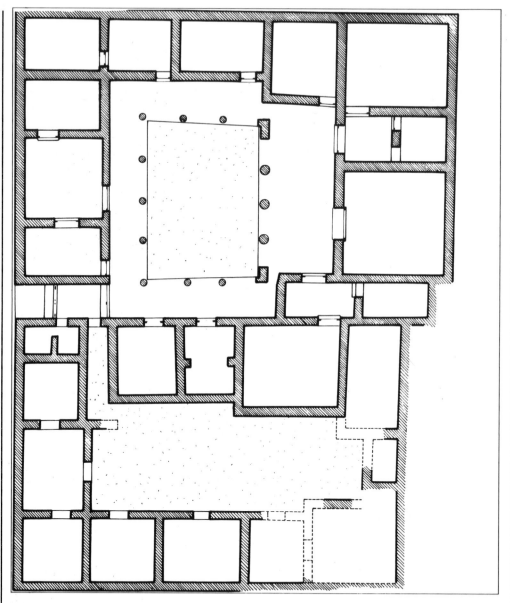

**FORM 12** *Type of peristyle house formed by joining two separate Priene houses*

tion of the remains, one sees that two separate houses of the megaron type had later been joined together. It is certain that this alteration was made in the 2nd century BC when columns were the fashion.

Two important buildings situated in these blocks of houses have been described under the temples as they have a sacred identity (see the temples of Cybele and Alexander the Great).

*The Byzantine church situated to the south of the theatre, 6 century AD.*

# THE BYZANTINE BUILDINGS

In the Byzantine period Priene was a bishopric. Findings and inscriptions indicate that the city was completely deserted after Emperor Andronicus II Palaiologos (1282-1328).

During this period, a great part of the walls were restored and fortified, while aqueducts and reservoirs were rebuilt .The building, situated in the north-east corner within the temenos area of the Zeus Temple, was used a citadel (Plan-I; 22).

The real citadel however was the one in the Acropolis, of which the ramparts and towers are visible, and the areas to protect were densely clustered in the northern region of Mycale.

Numerous Byzantine buildings within the city have been demolished to reveal buildings from ealier periods.

A preserved church stands to the theatre. The Byzantine church situated to the south of the theatre, 6 century A D. Understood to be the church of the Archbishdopric, the edifice was built in the 6th century AD. The church, 26.65 metres long and 4.28 metres wide, comprises three wings (Plan-I; 23). The middle nave is separated from the others by the rows of Doric columns on its sides. The apse has not been completely excavated. The steps leading to the ambo in the middle nave can still be seen. Here are also seats for the archbishop and the priests. The floor of the church was with inscriptions and certain other architectural elements belonging to the Athena Temple.

It is understood that the church originally had a flat roof, and that a dome was added later with the construction of piers.

The narthex has two doors. The small building, between the Athena Temple and the church is believed to be the baptistery (Plan-I; 24).

# MILETUS

# MILETUS

## NAME-FOUNDATION-HISTORY

The name, which is Miletos in the Ionic dialect and Milatos in the Doric one, is said to be related to the city of Milatos situated on the island of Crete.

The idea is widespread that the Kingdom of Ahhiyava, mentioned in written Hittite documents and of which the location is as yet unknown, was founded in the region of Miletus, and the city of Millavanda also mentioned in the same source is identified with Miletus.

The geographer Strabo and the historian Epheros have written that the city was first founded by Cretans, whereas according to Homer it was founded by Carians. That Miletus was founded in the 10th century BC at the end of the Greek migrations, by Ionians under the direction of Neleus, son of King Codros of Athens, is still another hypothesis.

Excavations undertaken around the Athena temple in the years 1955 to 1957 revealed megaron-type houses, and protective walls of a width of 4 metres belonging to the Mycenaean (1400 BC)settlement as well as fragments of Mycenaean ceramics.

According to findings acquired in recent years during the research work at Killik Tepe in the south of Akköy and dated back to pre-Mycenaean periods, the founding date of the city goes as far back as the 11th century BC. From the results of excavations and research up to the present day, it is accepted that the former indigenous people of the region (Carians), became integrated with the latecomers, the Cretans, and had founded an important Mycenaean city in Miletus. This earliest of the settlements, the Mycenaean city, as shown by the findings, was in the precincts of the Athena temple.One can also see here findings and remains from the Geometric and Archaic periods.

All these findings give us the idea that Miletus was not only an Anatolian city containing Mycenaean export articles, but was a Mycenaean colony enjoying close cultural relations with Greece and Crete.

It is understood from the structure of the city walls revealed in the excavations that the Archaic city acropolis was on the hill of Kalabaktepe.

Our insufficient knowledge of these periods will gain in clarity only in the continuation of the excavations and research.

Although situated on extremely fertile and arable land, Miletus, instead of being an agricultural and livestock raising area, gave navigation foremost importance, and from the year 670 BC began colonization movements. It established a great number of colonies on the coasts of the Black Sea, the Mediterranean and the Marmara Sea. Pliny states in his work "Naturalis Historia" that Miletus had founded about 90 colonies. However it is quite certain that some of these were in the form of small coastal markets (Emporiums). The most important among the Milesian colonies were naucratis (on the Egyptioan coast), Sinope, Amisos, Abydos, Cyzicos and Olbia.

Due to the contribution of its markets extending from Egypt to the Black Sea, Miletus made substantial progress in maritime commerce, the city prospered and became the leader eof Ionia both in political and cultural spheres.

At the end of the 7th century BC, Miletus ensured its own protection from the continuous assults of the Lydian Kingdom, by making a treaty with the Lydians through the rational rule of the famous dictator Thrasybulus, and continued the colonization movement.

After the Kingdom of Lydia fell to the Persian king Cyrus in 546 BC, the fear that Persian rule would expand brought all Ionian cities together again under the Panionion League. Following discussions, defence preparations against the Persians were begun, and also help was asked from the Spartans. In spite of all these measures however, the cities were not able to defend themselves against the Persians, and beginning with Ephesus, they almost all came under Persian rule.

However miletus, again acting politically, signed a treaty with the Persian king Cyrus similar to the one it had made with the Kingdom of Lydia, and stopped the Persians from besieging the city.

Severe constraint and excessive customs charges under Persian rule which lasted until 500 BC, resulted in limiting overseas trade which led all Ionian cities to economic crisis. Miletus, although maintaining its semi-autonomous status due to the treaty made with the Persians, was the city the most affected by the economic crisis. The fact that the straits and the coasts of the Marmara and Black Sea which connected it to the colonies were under Persian rule, had reduced substantially the income it obtained through overses trade. Aristagoras, who at the time ruled over the city and who was of an ambitious personality, arranged with the cooperation of the satrapy of Sardis, an attack on the island of Naxos with a view to making new efforts in overseas trade. At the end of the unsuccessful attack which lasted four months, Aristagoras, thinking his authority shaken, in an effort to withdraw attention from the defeat, forced the people, by inciting them, to revolt against the Persians. The revolt which Aristagoras, ignoring the opposition of Hecataeus, started with the objective of showing himself as the rescuer of Ionian cities, soon spread to all the other cities, headed by Miletus, under Persian constraint.

Help from other states was need to withstand the Persians who were very strong. There was no answer from Athens and Sparta to Aristagosas' demand for help. The revolt, which lasted six years and which at first seemed to be successful, ended in 494 BC with a disastrous defeat of the Ionian fleet by the Persians in front on the island of Lade. Miletus and Chios were the cities most affected by the aftermath of the battle of Lade. The Persians besieged Miletus by land and sea, and completely razed, destroyed and sacked it. They drove the people away to everything and who were enslaved, this was the beginning of terrible times. The sad end of Miletus affected the writer of tragedies, Phrynichus, and caused him to write a play with the title of "The Capture of Miletus". The play was staged in Athens in 492 BC. However, it was banned and the author punished, because of the excessive reaction of the people.

Miletus played an important role in the defeat of the Persians in the battle of Mycale in 479 BC. Miletus joined in 477 the Sea League of Attica-Delos, established shortly after the battle, and paind 10 talents for the period 450-459. Membership dues paid to the League were proportionate to the economic structure of the cities. For example, the 10 talents paid by Miletus when Ephesus, one of the most important cities of Ionia, was paying 7.5 talents, show that the city had regained its old prosperity.

In 442 BC, after the Samos-Priene war, Pericles reduced by half the customs taxes paid by Miletus to the League, with a view to enabling Miletus to have closer relations with Athens, and to stimulate overseas trade. As a consequence of this, at the beginning of the Peloponnesian war Miletus was on the side of Athens and acted as its protector. After the Peloponnesian war which lasted some thirty years, the Sicilian campaign caused Athens to suffer great losses and its economy to be upset. To secure economic aid, Athens contacted the Persian satrap and told him that if aid was provided he would allow the cities on the western Anatolian coast to come under Persian rule. Thus, the two hostile nations negotiated a treaty and Miletus came under Persian rule again.

The Persian satrap Tissaphernes, commissioned to rule over Miletus, built himself a castle in the vicinity of the theatre and settled down in the city. His first action was to make Miletus leave the Attice-Delos Sea League (412 BC). He continued to rule over the city until the year 401 BC.

In later years, Miletus came under the rule of the Carian satraps Hekatomnus and Mausolus, and after the death of Mausolus in 353 DC it was again ruled by Athens.

A new are started when Alexander the Great defeated the Persians in the Battle of the Granicus (the battle of the riders - 334 BC) and took over all the Ionian cities without encountering any difficulty. When Alexander besieged Miletus, the city was headed by the Persian satrap Hegesistratus, who, although a Persian, carried a Greek name, withstood the armies of Alexander, but Alexander captured the part of the city remaining outside the walls (Kalabaktepe) and took up temporary quarters there with his army. Although later a naval attack was attempted, the city was in a short time defeated by Alexander's powerful army and fleet, and had to surrender. The city walls were greatly damaged during the resistance. When Alexander seized Miletus, he forgave the people, substituted a people's rule for oligarchy, abolished the taxes paid to the Persians, and started re-instating activities in the city. During this period Miletus attained a high development rate and revived. It began regaining commercial importance through its colonies and the new markets it acquired in the East.

After the death of Alexander (314 BC) and the battle of Ipsus (301 BC), Miletus came under the rule of the Kingdom of Selecucus, and during the reigns of Seleucus I and his son Antiochus I the city was again active in building. Lysimachus, a commander under Alexander, who took over the rule in 287 BC, played an important role in the development of the city He contributed greatly to its prosperity by the donation he made circa 295 BC. During the Helenistic period, Miletus came at intervals under the influence and rule of the kingdoms of the Ptolemies, Seleucus and Pergamum, and gained autonomy with the treaty of Apameia (188 BC) made following the battle of Magnesia ad Sipylum During this period, the city was in close relationship with the Kingdom of Pergamum, and a gymnasium and a stadium were built with the donation of Eumenes II, King of Pergamum.

In 133 BC, in conformity with the will of Attalus III of Pergamum, the Anatolian lands were attached to Rome. The cities which came under the Roman system of "Provincia Asia" in 129 BC, were preparing for revolt because of the excessivity of Roman taxes and the attacks of pirates Mithradates, King of Pontus, took advantage of this situation and was received as a saviour when he came to West Anatolian cities which were displeased with Roman rule All Roman citizens resident in the province of Asia (about 80,000 people) were massacred in one day, in the revolt started under the leadership of Mithradates

However the revolt was subdued shortly afterwards with the intervention of Rome Mithridates was punished by Sulla who took over the rule again. In the year 63 BC Miletus sided with the Romans in the war against the pirates, which resulted in victory, and gained sympathy from Rome because of the help it provided, the city received special attention from the Roman Emperors In 38 BC, with the recognition of it beeing autonomous, Miletus once again made a good progress and reached the level of metropolis throughout Ionian cities. Good relations begun with Augustus continued through the periods of Tiberius, Trajan, Antoninus Pius, and Septimus Severus. Many monumental structures such as the theatre, the baths of Faustina and Capito, the Nymphaneum, and the north gate of the South Agora were built during this period. Starting with the 3rd century AD, this brilliant period began to gradually decline. The city began to be abandoned as the harbours silted up, the surrounding area turned into marshland and malaria reached dangerous proportions.

In the Byzantine period, the city boundaries were quite reduced, and buildings were mostly clustered around the theatre. The walls were rebuilt and some buildings were restored. Efforts made towards progress in the 6th century AD did not last long.

The region was subjected to Turkish assaults after the battle of Malazgirt (1071) and gradually weakened. On coins issued by the Menteşe emir (prince) Orhan Bey in his name, the city is mentioned as Palatia. Miletus later came under the rule of the Principality of Menteşeoğulları, founded in 1279 in the Carian region, and it retained that status until the Ottoman period The city flourished again under the Menteşe emir Ilyas Bey and a great number of baths and mosques were built The name of Palatia was changed into Balat. There was also a revival in commerce during this period.

In 1424 Balat was taken inside the boundaries of the Ottoman Empire by Murat II. During the time that elapsed until the proclamation of the Republic, the city gradually turned into a village and was completely abandoned in the 17th century.

The village of Balat, lying within the ruins of Miletus, was destroyed completely in the earthquake of 1955 and was moved into the new settlement area, about 1 km to the south of Miletus. A big section of the new village of Balat lies on top of the necropolis.

# EXCAVATIONS AND RESEARCH WORK

Research on Miletus began in 1446 with the traveller Cyriacus. Evliya Çelebi who visited the city in 1670, stated in his work "The Book of Travels", that Miletus, which once took its place as being among the most important cities of the ancient world, was completely in ruins.

Publications found indicate that research work had been carried out by various scientists in the beginnings of the 17th, 18th and 19th centuries.

B Haussoullier, O Rayet and A Thomas, who made excavations in the Didymaion, are also among the persons who participated in research work on Miletus.

The plan of the city was first drawn by C Humann.

Excavations were first begun in 1899 under Th. Weigand for the Berlin Museum. Excavation work, interrupted during the First World War, was later carried on under Carl Weickert and G Kleiner. At present, excavations and restoration work are going on under the supervision of Professor Dr. Müller Wiener for the German Institute of Archaeology.

# THE LOCATION AND PLAN OF THE CITY

## (Plan-II)

Miletus, situated near the village of Balat in the present district of Söke and no longer a harbour city, was founded on a peninsula, approximately 2.5 km long. The peninsula had four harbours, three on the west side,

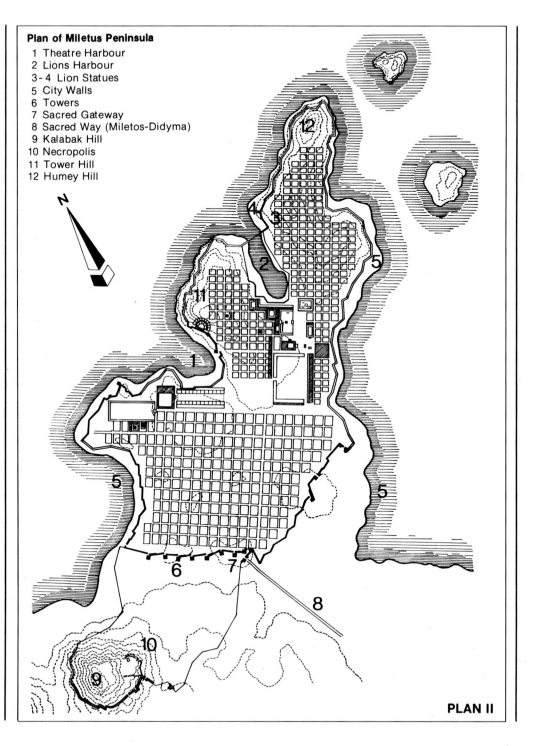

**Plan of Miletus Peninsula**

1 Theatre Harbour
2 Lions Harbour
3-4 Lion Statues
5 City Walls
6 Towers
7 Sacred Gateway
8 Sacred Way (Miletos-Didyma)
9 Kalabak Hill
10 Necropolis
11 Tower Hill
12 Humey Hill

**PLAN II**

and one on the east. The harbours on the west, mentioned in archeological literature as the Lions' Theatre and Athena Harbours, were better situated for protection.

Because of its narrow entrance, the Lions' Harbour was the most suitable for protection. The harbour, named after the stone lions on either side of its entrance, is at present completely silted up and has become marshland. The lions' statues, symbolically guarding the harbour, were made in the Hellenistic period and still stand in their original places. The West Harbour, lying just in front of the theatre, to the south of the Athena Temple and to the east of the island of Lade, is also silted up with alluvial mud brought by the Maeander river.

When the city was rebuilt after the defeat by the Persians in 494 BC, the settlement was clustered around the Lions Harbour.

The plan of the city was designed by Hippodamus of Miletus, arcihtect and town planner. It is known that Hippodamus and first applied to his home city the grid plan which he had developed on inspiration from geometrically designed settlements, and that later many cities were laid out according to this plan. Miletus, which is a fine example of the grid plan, comprises houses on blocks created by streets and side streets crossing at right angles, with public buildings in the city centre, This plan retained in the Hellenistic period, however in the Roman period it began to deteriorate gradually and inevitably. The remains of the city of Miletus, which suffered great destruction caused by wars, earthquakes, silting up of harbours, and each period destroying the one before, display quite a complex structure. Almost in every building characteristics of different periods can be seen.

# THE CITY WALLS

Miletus, where for centuries very different settlements and cultures had existed, displays wall remains which differ widely in construction and location.

The remains from the earliest walls lie under the foundations of the Athena Temple and date from the years 1600-1400 BC. These will be mentioned with the Athena Temple.

A section of the Archaic walls was uncovered in the lower parts of the south and south-east slopes of the hill of Kalabaktepe. These walls indicate two separate periods as their construction techniques are different. The southern walls were constructed in poligonal technique and can be dated back to 650 BC. The fact that one does not come across early Archaic walls in the lower city indicates that Miletus was at this time not protected by walls, and that in the defence of the city, Kalabaktepe Hill played an important role as its acropolis. To the south-east of the hill, wall remains made of stone blocks can be dated back to 550 BC according to their construction technique. The remains of a tower and city walls running just in front of the theatre are also understood to have been built at the same date, which fact is evidence that the whole city was in this period surrounded by walls.

After the disaster of 494 BC, Miletus could not recover for a long time. However, in the intense reconstruction work which was begun in the 3rd century BC, the walls were also worked on. The construction of the Hellenistic walls were continued into the 2nd century BC. A section of these can be seen to the south of the Lions Harbour and to the west of the stadium, and a beautiful example is in front of the theatre. The southern extension of the walls was uncovered in the excavations and nine towers were identified in this section of about 500 metres. Standing at 60 meter-intervals, the towers each had a separate door and were of a very strong construction. The 8th and 9th towers standing closer together give evidence of the existence of a gate in between them (the Sacred Gate). One other gate of the city lies in the direction of the south-east corner of the South Agora.

In the Roman period, the Sacred Gate was rebuilt and certain sections of the walls were repaired.

The really important change in the walls is seen in the Byzantine period. In this period, as the harbours had completely turned into marshland, the city boundaries were kept quite small and the walls were rebuilt in accordance with these boundaries. Architectural elements from a great number of buildings of Miletus were used as construction material for the Early Byzantine walls, which according to inscriptions were built by Justinian in 538 AD.

# THE SACRED GATE
# (The south gate of the city)

This gate, standing in the central part of the walls surrounding the south of Miletus, was the starting point of the Sacred Road leading to the Apollo Temple in Didyma. This is the reason for which it was named "the Sacred Gate".

The 5 meter wide monumental gate with strong towers on each side displays different periods. The uncovered remains of the Sacred Gate madde it clear that, beginning with the Archaic period, and going through the Hellenistic into the Roman periods the gate was rebuilt on top of the structure of the previous period. Today a great part of the gate is covered by earth and cannot be seen. During the restoration of the Sacred Road. Emperor Trajan had the Sacred Gate built

too. The foundations of the gate built in the Roman period lie 1 meter above the Hellenistic one. It is understood from an inscription on the entrance of the gate that the construction of the Sacred Gate, begun in 100 AD, was completed a year later.

# THE NECROPOLIS

In various places in Miletus there are necropoli of extremely differing types and periods. However, the region where tombs are in intensity, lies on the lower slopes of the hills of Kalabaktepe and Değirmentepe. The region is bounded by the hill of Kaçartepe. The earliest tombs belong to the Mycenaean period; these tombs lying on the lower parts of the north-east slopes of Değirmentepe and Kalabaktepe face east. Necropoli of the Archaic, Classic, Hellenistic and Roman periods lie on the lower parts of the south and south-west slopes of Kalabaktepe in the direction of the Sacred Gate. Numerous examples of these tombs in the form of tombs cut into rocks, chamber tombs sarcophagi are at present visible.

Tombs in the form of Heroon (Monumental tombs) were generally built for important persons and administrators. These lie in the centre of the city.

The Necropolis, extending over a large area from the region between the Delphinion and Derviş Tekkesi on the north-east of the city, to the lower slopes of Humeytepe, was used during the periods of the Menteşeoğulları and the Ottoman Empire. Another cemetery dating from the same period lies within the courtyard of the Ilyas Bey Mosque and around it. Fine examples of tombstones with inscriptions and of various types can be seen in the courtyard of the mosque and in the museum in Miletus.

Certain findings around the modern cemetery lying in the region of the stadium and the Heroon, indicate that it was also used in the Ottoman period.

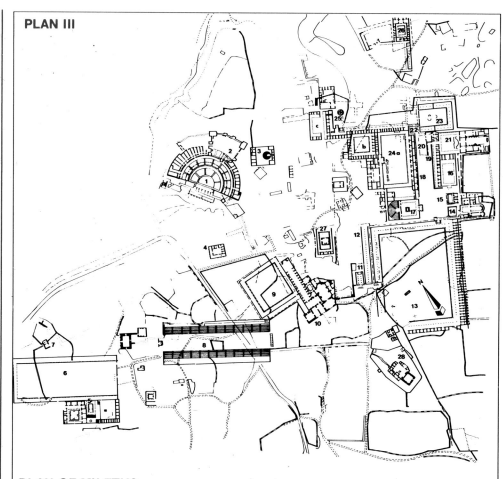

## PLAN III

## PLAN OF MILETUS

1 THEATRE
2 BYZANTINE CHURCH
3 HEROON
4 CARAVANSERAI
5 TEMPLE OF ATHENA
6 WEST AGORA
7 HEROON
8 STADIUM
9 GYMNASIUM
10 FAUSTINA BATHS
11 TEMPLE OF SERAPIS
12 DEPOT BUILDING
13 SOUTH AGORA
13 a) NORTH GATE OF AGORA
14 BYZANTINE CHURCH

15 MONUMENTAL FOUNTAIN (NYMPHAION)
16 HELLENISTIC GYMNASIUM
17 BOULEUTERION
18 SACRED WAY
19 IONIC STOA
20 MENTESHE BATHS
21 BATHS OF VERGILIUS CAPITO
22 HARBOUR GATEWAY
23 DELPHINION
24 a, b, c, - NORTH AGORA
25 HARBOUR MONUMENT
26 ROMAN BATHS
27 HEROON
28 ILYAS BEY MOSQUE AND COMPLEX

*Parados wall and vaulted door.*

*The Theatre, 4th century BC. - 2nd century AD.*

# THE THEATRE

## (Plan-III; 1)

The Theatre, erected on the south-west slopes of the hill of Kaletepe, profiting from the natural inclination, is the best preserved building of Miletus. First erected in the 4th century BC it has taken its present form by later alterations undergone in the Hellenistic, Roman and Byzantine periods. The theatre which could seat 5,300 spectators in the Hellenistic period, reached a capacity of 25,000 seats in the Roman period (2nd century AD).

Like all other ancient theatres, the theatre of Miletus consisted of the stage building, the orchestra and the cavea (seats of the spectators). In the front part of the theatre there are Archaic and Hellenistic wall remains, and in the direction of the proscenium the remains of an Archaic tower. The Byzantine walls, running over the proscenium, have ruined the stage building.

The facade, facing the harbour, of the theatre is 140 metres long. Whereas the entrance on the east side, has no stairs, the entrance on the west side because of the insufficiency of the inclination of the ground was built with stairs. The base parts of the parados walls have mouldings, the workmanship of the west side has been completed, whereas that of the west side has been left incomplete.

To the 34 meter wide und two-storeyed

*The Theatre, 4th century BC. - 2nd century AD.*

*The Theatre 4th century BC.   2nd century AD.*

69

*The base standing in the orchestra. The tripod cauldron and reliefs of griffons.*

*Egg-and dart molding, 4th century BC.*

*Hunting scene on a fragment of the reliefs decorating the stage building 2nd century AD.*

stage building one more floor was added in the Roman period, thus making it a three-storeyed building. It is understood from various fragments found, that in this period the stage was very richly decorated with columns, pilaster capitals, statues and reliefs. A great number of the findings can be seen in front of the theatre. The reliefs depict hunting scenes of Eros.

The upper part of the cavea was supported by vaulted galleries as the height of the hill on which it leaned was not sufficient. The height of the cavea would thus have reached 40 metres, and it is certain that from the top seats one had a view of the sea. The cavea consisted of three sections, each of which had nineteen stepped rows of seats. In the exact centre of the first section was a box of honour reserved for the emperors, which was separated by four columns. Two of the columns can be seen in their original places. The cavea also included perpendicular stairs, termed kirkides, to enable the spectators to reach their places easily. Two diozomas dividing the cavea and vaulted galleries connected to these by doors, facilitated the entrances and exits. The stones of the theatre were used as construction material for the building of the Byzantine citadel, situated on the upper central part of the rows of seats.

*Head of gorgon, the stage building.*

This caused the upper part of the cavea to be completely destroyed. The entrance and exit to the theatre were made through the arched doors in the parados walls, and the stepped galleries connected to them. Apart from the entrance and exit doors on the east, west and the upper part of the cavea, the passage extending on the west side, from the top row of seats to the lowest one, was built to facilitate the exits. The high arched doors in the parados walls and the galleries were decorated with pilaster capitals.

*Reliefs representing Eros hunting, the stage building, 2nd century AD.*

*Example of pilaster capitals of vaulted gates, 2nd century AD.*

# THE BYZANTINE CITADEL

## (Plan-III; 2)

The extant walls and the tower standing on the cavea of the theatre, are the walls for the citadel built in the Byzantine period. The citadel walls, widening slightly towards the north-east, have been fortified with turrets and towers. At the ends of the wide side walls are two big towers, and in the centre are two turrets. The citadel has two gates, one on the east the other on the west, and on either side of the west gate, which is considered to be the main gate are towers.

The citadel was used in the periods of the Principality of Menteşe and the Ottomans with certain changes effected.

# THE HEROON (Monumental Tomb)

## (Plan-III; 3)

This structure lying in a east-west direction on the slope east of the theatre, is a Heroon erected to dedicate to an important person. The monumental tomb, built in the Hellenistic period, is greatly ruined due to changes effected in the Roman period. The building comprises rooms on the east and west sides, and a courtyard in the centre. Two of the rooms have floors with mosaics made of pebbles. Ionic capitals and the entablature elements reflect Hellenistic period characteristics. The tomb chamber stands in the centre of the tumulus-shaped round section in the courtyard, and is

*Entrance of the Heroon near the Theatre, Hellenistic*

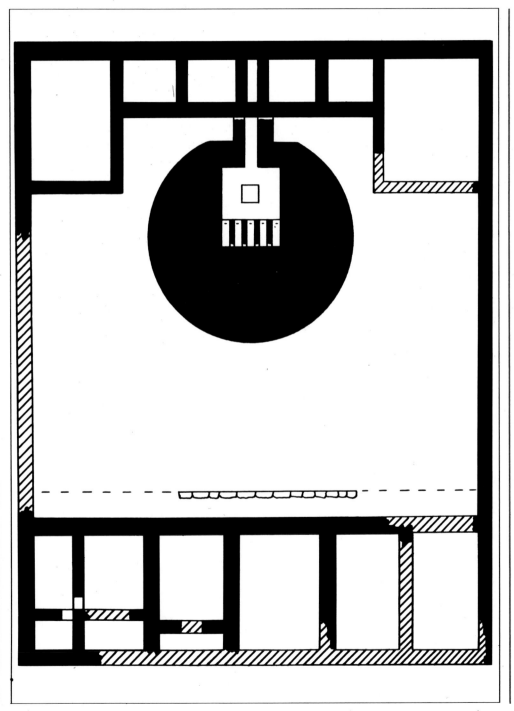

**FORM 13** *Plan of Monumental Tomb (Heroon) next to the Theatre*

*Tomb cabins inside the Heroon.*

reached by a short, arched dromos from the east side. On the west side of the square (2 metres by 2 metres) vaulted tomb chamber are five little tomb chambers lying side by side (Form-13). The tomb partitions are believed to be made of kline. In the exact centre of the tomb chamber there is a quadrangular sacrificial hole. It is beyond doubt that the Heroon was built in honour of a very important person in Miletus and his family, but who it was is not yet known for certain.

*The Caravanserai (inside view), 15th century AD.*

# THE CARAVENSERAI

# (Plan-III; 4)

The caravanserai, located to the south-east of the theatre, was built in the 15th century during the period of the Principality of Menteşe. It comprises a courtyard and rooms for lodging. The lower floor of the two-storeyed building was used as stables, and the upper floor to lodge travellers. The entrance to the 30-meter-long and 24-meter-wide building is in the north. To the north of the courtyard are the stairways leading to the second floor which is completely destroyed. Due to restoration work undertaken in recent years, the Caravanserai has lost all its original character.

In the direction of the south-east end of the eastern parados wall of the theatre there are the remains of a small bath, also built in the period of the Principality of Menteşe.

# THE ATHENA TEMPLE AND ITS ENVIRONS

## (Plan-III; 5)

Of the Athena Temple, located in the south-west of the city to the south of the theatre, and which is one of the earliest buildings of Miletus, only the foundations of the podium are in sight today. The building, erected on a north-south axis, conforms to the grid plan. The temple, 18 metres wide and 30 metres long, rested on a high podium and had stairs in the front ( the south ). No remains could be found of these stairs. In the central part of the podium, foundations of rough stone are the foundations of the square-shaped naos where the cult statue stood, and just in front are those of the pronaos. Each of the long sides of the peristasis had ten columns, the rear facade had seven and the front facade had six. The fewer number of columns in the front facilitated the entrance and exit. Fragments of Ionic capitals and architraves found in the excavations and now in the Miletus Museum, show that the temple was built in the Ionic order. According to the characteristics of these fragments and ceramic findings the temple has been dated back to the first half of the 5th century BC. Excavations in the environs of the Athena Temple have uncovered the earliest artifacts of Miletus. The remains around the temple constitute layers of different periods, merged into one another.

In the years 1955-57, K Weickert came across late Mycenaean (1400 BC) walls, which extended just to the south of the temple in an east-west direction and were 4 metres wide. These walls, of which a part can be seen today at the south-west corner of the Athena Temple, were fortified with towers. The lower parts of the thick walls display an earlier period technique. These parts of the walls, made of rubble, have the characteristics of Minos ( Crete ) culture, and can be dated back to 1600 BC. These excavations also revealed vestiges of dwellings of the Mycenaean period.

The remains on the left side of the Athena Temple belong to a large house of the Hellenistic period. It is understood that the marble-walled house was changed into a house with a peristyle in the Roman period ( 3rd century AD ).

In excavations carried out on the south side of the Athena Temple in 1963, the foundations of another temple, erected on an east-west axis and dated back to the 7th century BC, were uncovered.

All these excavations revealed, besides remains from the Cretan, Mycenaean, Geometric and Archaic periods, also ceramic findings from the same periods. Fine examples of these ceramics can be seen in the archaeological museums, in Istanbul and Izmir. The findings, and remains give evidence that the area and surroundings of the Athena Temple was the oldest settlement areas of Miletus ( Form-14 ).

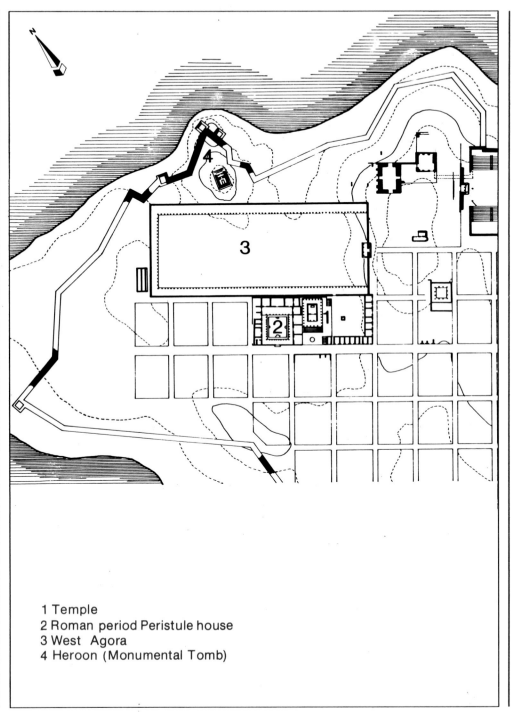

1 Temple
2 Roman period Peristule house
3 West Agora
4 Heroon (Monumental Tomb)

**FORM 14 Temple of Athena and environment**

# THE WEST AGORA
## (Plan-III; 6)

To the north of the Athena Temple lies the West Agora, of incomplete excavation, but of which the plan has been determined by borings. The building, lying on an east-west axis, measures 191 metres by 79 metres, and is surrounded by porticoes on three sides. Column bases and shafts, and a cornice fragment from the entablature indicate that the agora was built in the Ionic style. According to the ceramic findings, it was established that the agora was built in the Hellenistic period. On the upper part of the agora is a cemetery.

# THE HEROON
# (Monumental Tomb)
## (Plan-III; 7)

On a little hill to the north of the agora there are the remains of a monumental tomb (heroon). The building consisted of a vaulted tomb chamber, rising on a high podium with steps on the north side. It is understood that the vaulted tomb chamber was added to the building of Hellenistic character in the Roman period. The edifice, undergoing numerous alterations in the Roman and Seljuk periods, was completely destroyed in the earthquake of 1955.

The high walls standing in the olive grove to the north-east of the West Agora are the remains of a Roman bath. However, there is no definite knowledge of its plan as the excavation is not completed.

# THE STADIUM
## (Plan-III; 8)

A great part of the stadium which was built in conformity with the grid plan, profiting from the natural lay of the land south of the Theatre Harbour, is covered by earth. However, its plan was determined by exploratory trenches and it is understood from an inscription of dedication on the west side walls that it was built in the 2nd century BC by Eumenes II.

The revealed remains display mostly characteristics of the Roman period, which give evidence that the building was reconstructed in the Roman period with substantial repairs.

lying on an east-west axis, the stadium measures 191 metres by 129.5 metres and has a capacity of about 15,000 persons. The building consists of two wings with an area for running in the middle. Each wing has twenty stepped rows of seats, supported in the rear by walls. In the east corner of the

**FORM 15** *East Gate of Stadium (Reconstruction)*

northern seats, one can see a part of the wall built in the Hellenistic period. A door in this section leads through a stepped and vaulted passage to the rows of seats. The shorter sides of the stadium are, in contrast with the Roman examples of horseshoe shape, angular, and have monumental gates in them. The western gate with its facade onto the stadium, was, according to architectural elements found, built in the Hellenistic period. In the hall reached by steps, Ionic columns carried the pedimented entablature.

The eastern gate built in the Roman period, with its very ostentatious structure, had the appearance of a triumphall arch. A double row of sixteen high based (postament) columns carried the quite richly decorated entablature. Arches stood over Corinthian capitals and on the top was a roof. It is believed that this magnificent gate, with seven entrances, of which the middle one was wider, was used mostly for celebrations and ceremonies (Form-15).

# THE GYMNASIUM
## (Plan-III; 9)

It is stated in an inscription on a circular statue pedestal taken to Berlin during excavations before the Republic, that King Eumenes II of Pergamum (196-160 BC) had a gymnasium built for Milesians. The inscription on the stadium wall also bears evidence that the edifice had been built by Eumenes II. It is accepted from this data that, as in the Priene example, Miletus also, had a gymnasium which constituted a complex with the Stadium. Its Palaestra, 62 metres wide and 64 metres long, is adjacent to the north-east corner of the stadium, but no door providing the connection to the Stadium could be found. The north-east corner of the

palaestra, surrounded by columned porticoes, was discovered during excavations. Column bases and capitals seen in this section are in the Corinthian style. Because of alterations undergone in the Roman and Byzantine periods, the gymnasium displays a complex structure. There is a big door at the east corner of the northern portico, and in the east portico are doors connecting to the Faustina Baths. To the south of the palaestra are the remains of another columned portico.

# THE FAUSTINA BATHS
## (Plan-III; 10)

This buildings, understood from inscriptions found during excavations to have been built by the wife of Emperor Marcus Aurelius, Faustina, (161-180 BC) was named after her. A greater part of the baths, with a layout contrary to the grid plan, has been uncovered. The edifice is in quite good condition and, like all Roman baths, consists of the dressing-room (Apodyterium), cold room (Frigidarium), warm room (Tepidarium), hot room (Calidarium), steam room (Sudatorium), boiler room and exercise area (Palaestra) (Form-16).

Baths played a very important part in the daily life of ancient Romans. Besides bathing, being massaged, and perspiring, various sports were practised and discussions on current events were held there. Thus a great part of the day was spent in the baths.

It is understood that the palaestra of the Eumenes II Gymnasium was used as the palaestra of the Faustina Baths after undergoing certain alterations. Three doors on the east side of this 77.5 meter wide and 79.41 meter long courtyard open onto the Apodyterium which is 80 metres long, with

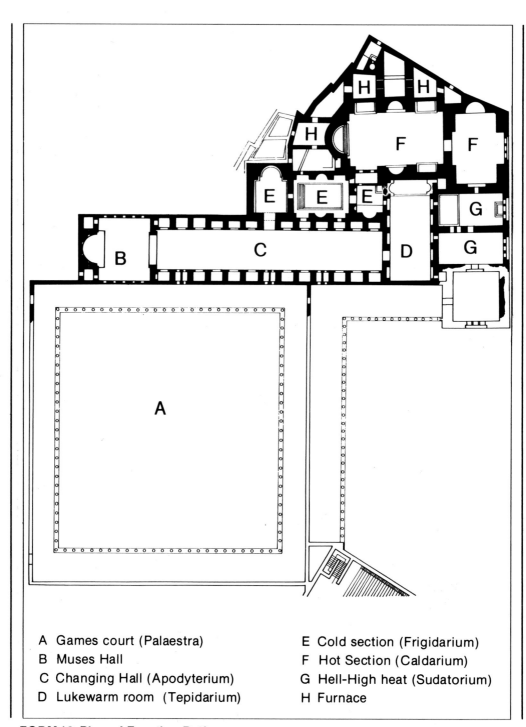

A Games court (Palaestra)
B Muses Hall
C Changing Hall (Apodyterium)
D Lukewarm room (Tepidarium)

E Cold section (Frigidarium)
F Hot Section (Caldarium)
G Hell-High heat (Sudatorium)
H Furnace

**FORM 16 Plan of Faustina Baths**

*The Faustina Baths and the Palaestra, 2nd century AD.*

*The Calidarium seen from the south*

*The undressing ball (Apodyterium) of the Faustina Baths.*

*The statue of the river god (Maindros) in the Frigidarium.*

*The Calidarium seen from the north*

undressing rooms (cabins) on both of its longer sides. Benches made for lying down and resting are visible in the rooms.To the north of the Apodyterium lies the section termed the Hall of the Muses.

Statues of Apollo, Asclepius, Telephorus, the nine Muses and a head of Aphrodite were found in this hall which has a large apse with four niches on the north wall and five niches on each of the side walls. Of these statues some are on display in the Archaeolagical Museum in İstanbul and some in the museums in Berlin. On either side of the apse there are two small rooms. In the Byzantine period entrance to the baths was provided by a door constructed in the room on the north-east corner.

Doors open from the Apodyterium onto the Tepidarium and the three partitioned Frigidarium. The latter is centrally situated with a big swimming pool. At the sides of the pool, one can see the statues of river gods (Maindrus) and lions which have remained in their original places. The Faustina Baths has two calidaria. The central calidarium which is the largest hall of the building measures 27.30 metres by 14.85 metres. It was covered by vaults and had a height of approximately 25 metres (Form-17). On the north wall of the hall is a large apse, and on the side walls are quadrangular niches. Sudatoria, the hottest sections of the baths, are situated at the south side. The intensity of the heating flues of the hypocaust system in the walls of the two sudatoria of similar dimensions are remarkable. Roman baths were heated by a system termed Hypocaust. The heating was provided by the circulation of heated air through wall flues of baked earth, and tiles laid in regular intervals below the marble floor. More than one boiler room must have been needed to heat baths of this size. Three boiler rooms were discovered to the north and east of the calidarium, the

**FORM 17** *Faustina Bath Caldarium (Reconstruction)*

hotter section of the baths, but the south part where the hottest sections would have not yet been excavated.

The Faustina Baths were repaired under Anastasius (491-518 AD) and then reopened for use.

*Milet'e cut! the Temple of Serapis*

*The pediment of the temple of Serapis with relief of Helios Serapis in the middle.*

# THE SERAPIS TEMPLE (Plan-III; 11)

The temple, lying between the Faustina Baths and the South Agora on a north-south axis is badly damaged. However, fragments discovered in the vicinity disclose information on the architecture of the temple. The Serapis Temple, built on a different plan, consists of the pronaos, the entrance to the building, and the rectangular haos, the chamber housing the cult statue. On the south side of the temple, the stepped and four columned prondos had the appearance of a propylaeum with an entablature which was the most ostentatious part of the temple. The column capitals indicate that the edifice was in the Corinthian style; the entablature, resting on the capitals, had a pediment. On the architrave is an inscription, and in the middle part of the pediment there is a relief of the god Helios Serapis wearing a crown of sunrays. The ceiling coffers were decorated with reliefs of the Muses and busts of gods. The naos, with two rows of columns dividing into three sections, gives the impression of a three naved Byzantine church. There were a total of ten columns in the naos which was 22.5 metres long and 12.5 metres wide. The columns had Attic-style bases and unfluted shafts. At the north side of the naos there was a special partition reserved for the cult statue. This temple, dedicated to the Egyptian god Serapis, displays the characteristics of two different periods. An inscription on the architrave mentions Julius Aurelius Menecles. The style of the inscription, showing characteristics of the 3rd century BC indicates that, the temple was rebuilt during the reign of Emperor Aurelius (270-275 AD) by the donation of Julius Aurelius Menecles.

# THE STOREHOUSE (Plan-III; 12)

This buildings, lying on a north-south axis along the western facades of the South Agora and the Bouleuterion is 163.4 meters long and 13.4 metres wide. Built in the Hellenistic period according to the remains, it was used as a granary (Form-18). It was used for the same purpose in the Roman period with certain changes. A row of columns running along the middle of the two-winged building, carried the roof. Column bases stood on angular and high stone blocks. The storehouse is believed to be connected to the South Agora by a door and a tunnel-like passage on the east side. A great latrine (toilet) was built between the storehouse and the South Agora in the Roman period, of which the only remains today are water closet holes and baked clay pipes.

*The storehouse, Hellenistic period.*

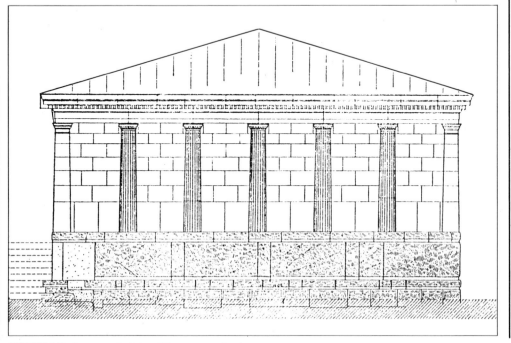

**FORM 18** *Storage Building (Reconstruction)*

# THE SOUTH AGORA
## (Plan-III; 13)

Just to the east of the south wall of the storehouse stands the western gate of the South Agora. Though not completely excavated, from parts uncovered by borings it has been determined that the agora was 196 metres long and 164 metres wide. The Hellenistic (2nd century BC) building is surrounded by stoas on all four sides. It has three gates, one each, on the north, west and south. The entire north gate was moved to Berlin, the south gate was destroyed during the construction of the Mosque of Ilyas Bey, and the west gate during the construction of the Byzantine walls. The north and west stoas do not have rows of shops. The stoas have double rows of columns in the Doric order, those in the front having shorter spaces between them. The shops lie in the rear sections of the east and south stoas. The east stoa has thirty nine pairs of shops, extending from north to south. These shops stand back to back, with some facing the street running outside it. The shops giving onto the agora have little stores at the rear, of the nineteen shops on the south, also, some open onto the agora and others onto the street outside. In the Roman period (mid. 2nd century AD), with numerous alterations, the agora was made into a very ostentatious building. Capitals in the Corinthian order in the stoas are findings of this period. It was also in this period that the agora gates took on the form of monumental structures. Particularly the North Gate opening onto the Ceremonial Street is one of the finest examples of facade architecture  However, because this magnificent gate was moved in its entirety to the Pergamum Museum in Berlin and is on display there, nothing but the remains of the podium can be seen in its place today. The two-storeyed gate is 14.71 metres high and 29 metres long. It rests on a high three-stepped podium and has three arched gates on the first floor. On the second floor, the arched gates change into niches with statues in each. The entablature, resting on columns with fluted shafts and Corinthian capitals, is richly decorated. The smaller proportioned columns of the upper floor carry the pediments. The frieze has a motif of garlands joined by bulls' heads whereas the ceiling coffers have geometric ornamentations.

# THE BYZANTINE CHURCH
## (Plan-III; 14)

This church, situated to the north of the South Agora, consists of an Atrium, a Narthex, a Baptistery and a Martyry, and has the appearance of a basilica. In the atrium are columns with Corinthian capitals and in the central part there are fountains. On the south side of the atrium, remains of Hellenistic walls can be seen. The three-naved main part has a double row of columns. Remains indicate that there was a bench for the choir to the north of the rows of columns and the ambo was in between them. In front of the apse stood a marble-topped bench for the priests. The martyry, adjacent to the south side of the apse, is in the shape of a clover leaf. The square-shaped baptistery lies on the north side of the atrium. The floor mosaics of the baptistery and church are on display in the museum in Miletus.

The church shows characteristics of two different periods. Initially built under Emperor Diocletian (284-305 AD), the church was rebuilt in the beginning of the 6th century AD in larger proportions. It was established from excavations that the church was built over Hellenistic houses.

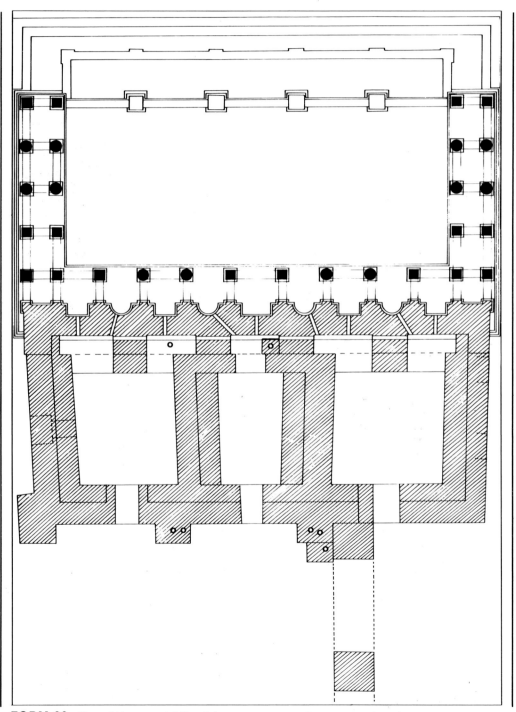

**FORM 20**  *Plan of Monumental Fountain*

*The monumental fountain (Nymphaneum), 2nd century AD.*

*The monumental fountain (Nymphaneum) reconstruction.*

# THE MONUMENTAL FOUNTAIN (NYMPHANEUM)

## (Plan-III; 15)

The monumental fountain in front of the Bouleuterion faces west. The three-storeyed structure is 17 metres high and 20 metres wide with a large pool in front. The edifice which was a fine example of facade arcihtecture is completely destroyed, with fragments scattered all around (Form-20). Today only the main division of the first floor, with the water tanks consisting of niches in front and three partitions in the rear, can be seen. One part of the Roman aqueduct providing water for the monumental founta-in, is behind it.

On all the floors of the marble-faced facade, Corinthian columns carried entablatures ending in pediments which had acroteria at the ends, and ornamentation consisting of volutes facing each other in the central sections. Statues of gods, goddesses and nymphs stood in the niches between the columns. Water flowed from amphorae held by statues on the first floor and from the mouths of fish at their sides into the pool in front. Of these statues some were taken to the Pergamum Museum in East Berlin, and some to the Archaeological Museum in Istanbul.

The fact that an inscription on the first floor mentions the name of Emperor Trajan (98-117 AD) and another on the second floor that of Emperor Gordian III (241-244 AD) indicates that the monumental fountain was erected in two different periods.

# THE HELLENISTIC GYMNASIUM

## (Plan-III; 16)

This Gymnasium, lying on a north-south axis to the north of the monumental fountain has its entrance, which is in the form of a propylaeum, on the south side. The stepped propylaeum, of a width of 5.5 metres, has four Ionic columns in front, two at the rear and a pediment. The entrance to the palaestra, formed into three passages by two Ionic columns, leads into the rectangular edifice surrounded by stoas on all sides. The columns of the north stoa, which contains five workrooms, are of the Ionic order. The style of arrangement of these rooms reminds one of the Priene gymnasium. The fact that the central room is larger than the others indicates this room to be the Ephebeion. The columns of the north stoa are placed with wider spaces between them, thus providing more light in the workrooms. The columns in the other stoas are in the Doric order. There are sixteen columns in the north-south direction. The gymnasium is known to have been built in the 2nd century BC because the axial system peculiar to the Hellenistic period was used in the gymnas-ium plan, and the ornamentation style of the fragments of roof elements found, showed Hellenistic characteristics.

# THE BOULEUTERION
# (Plan-III; 17)

The Bouleuterion where the Boule (Advisory Council) held its meetings consists of a propylaeum, a courtyard and an auditorium. The stepped propylaeum with four columns was built in the Corinthian style. The Corinthian capitals are amongst the earliest of their kind in Anatolia. On the friezes of the propylaeum, with four columns was built in the Corinthian style. The Corinthian capitals are amongst the earliest of their kind in Anatolia. On the friezes of the propylaeum, which had three doors with the central one larger, reliefs of war scenes are represented. These reliefs are a small model of the frieze which Eumenes II had ordered after the victory of Galatus.

The courtyard, 34.84 metres long and 29 metres wide, is surrounded on all sides by stoas with Doric columns. In the centre of the courtyard, there is a monumental tomb resting on a podium. The sides of the podium were decorated with motifs of garlands joined by bulls heads. This ornamentation cannot be seen because the monument, built in the Roman period, is almost completely destroyed (Form - 21a,b).

The meeting hall, with its appearance of a small theatre, can be entered by four doors in front. The semi-circular rows of seats (auditorium) have a capacity of about 1500 persons. There are two more doors on the west side. The doors are connected to the rows of seats with stepped passages. The walls of the first floor of the-storeyed building were built of squared blocks of marble, and the second floor was supported by half columns of the Doric order. On top of the columns rested the architrave with the frieze containing triglyphs and metopes above, and between the columns were windows. The wooden roof was supported by walls and four Ionic columns.

An inscription on the architrave of the

*The Bouleuterion, 2nd century BC.*

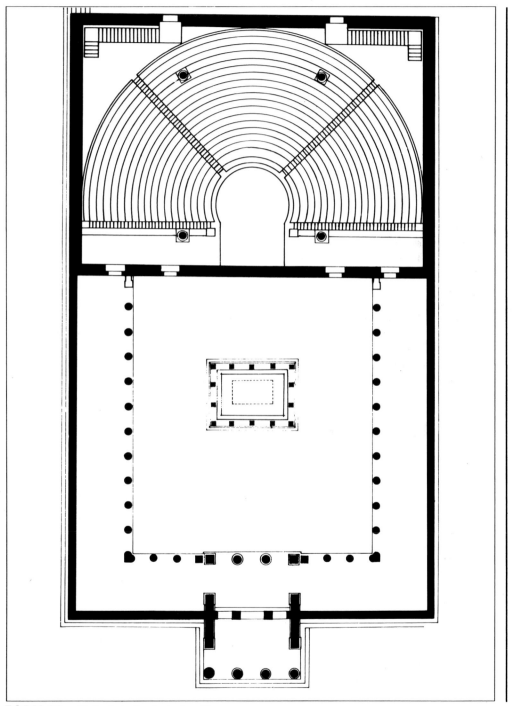

**FORM 21a** *Hellenistic Bouleuterion Plan*

**FORM 21b** *Bouleuterion (Reconstruction)*

entrance to the meeting hall states that the Bouleuterion was built by the donations of two brothers from Miletus, Timarchus and Heracleides, and that it was dedicated to King Antiochus IV. This shows that the Bouleuterion was built between the years 175 and 163 BC.

Two very important pieces discovered at the Bouleuterion excavations were taken to the Pergamum Museum in Berlin. One of these is a tripod cauldron with legs in the form of lions' paws and with decorations of palmetto motifs and mask reliefs on its surface, and the other is a fragment of a statue bearing the signature of the famous sculptor Anaximandros.

# THE SACRED WAY
# (Plan-III; 18)

This spectacular Sacred Way built in the Roman period was connected to the Harbour Gate and the Lions' Harbour, therefore foreign visitors coming to Miletus were greeted here by celebrations.

The Sacred Way, 100 metres long and 28 metres wide, began at the large square in front of the Bouleuterion and extended in a north-south direction. On both sides of it there were 5.75 meter wide sidewalks. The way was bounded on the west by the North Agora and there was an Ionic stoa on the east. Below the way ran the sewers.

*View of the Ionic stoa after the rain.|1st century AD.*

# THE IONIC STOA
## (Plan-III; 19)

The stoa, lying on a north-south axis to the east of the Sacred Way, had thirty five Ionic columns in front and nineteen shops at the rear. The backs of the shops were bounded by the Hellenistic gymnasium and the palaestra of the Vergilius Capito Baths. The stoa, situated at a higher level than the Sacred Way, was reached by steps. The northern part of it was destroyed due to the bath constructed during the Menteşeoğulları period. The stoa was, on the evidence of inscriptions, built in 50 AD by Tiberius Claudius Sophanes.

*Door with bands of ornament, the Menteşe baths, 15th century AD.*

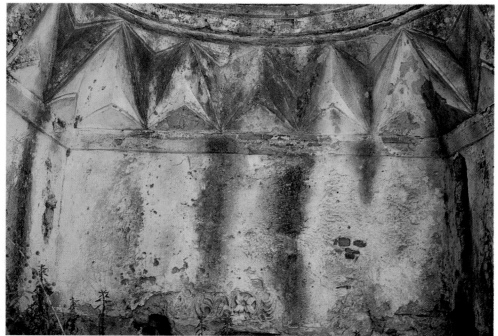
*Cupola with triangular motifs the Menteşe baths.*

# THE MENTEŞE BATHS

## (Plan-III; 20)

This buildings, standing adjacent to the Delphinion and to the north of the Ionic stoa, was built over the shops of the latter and is in quite good condition. The edifice, 17.85 metres wide and 24 metres long, can be entered by two doors on the west. The main divisions of the baths can be reached through the courtyard. Drawings of ships can be seen on the walls of the baths. The central section with the big dome is the hot room. The other divisions are distributed round the hot room. The transition from the square form into the dome is very well achieved with bands of ornamentation in the transition area. A half dome is used in some parts of the baths. The boiler room is on the south side, and has a separate door. The baths, built during the principality of Menteşe period, are at present used as a storehouse.

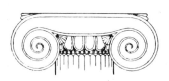

*The Vergilius Capito baths 41-54 AD.*

## THE VERGILIUS CAPITO BATHS

## (Plan-III; 21)

The palaestra of the baths which lie on an east-west axis to the north of the Hellenistic gymnasium, opens onto the Sacred Way. It is understood from an inscription on the architrave of the palaestra that it was built by Vergilius Capito who was commissioned in Anatolia during the reign of Claudius (41-54 AD). The squareshaped (38 x 38 metres) palaestra of the baths was surrounded by two-storeyed stoas in the Corinthian style. On the east side of the courtyard was a semi-circular pool. The entrance to the baths was also on this side, in the centre. In front is the three-partitioned tepidarium, and in the centre is the calidarium consisting of two partitions, placed one behind the other. In the north and south walls of the calidaria there are a number of semicircular and angular niches. The other parts of the baths are situated round the calidaria. The boiler room is in the south-east corner of the building.

## THE HARBOUR GATE

## (Plan-III; 22)

The monumental gate, located between the Delphinion and the Harbour Stoa, to the north of the Sacred Way, connected the city to the harbour. Understood from the remains to have been built in the first half of the 1st century AD, the building has a 3.84 meter wide passage in its central part. Double rows of columns on either side of this passage carried a flat roof. The marble-paved floor is at the same level as the Harbour Stoa.

*The Delphinium (The open air temple of Apollo Delphinius), archaic period.*

# THE DELPHINION
## The Open Air Temple of Apollo Delphinius

## (Plan-III; 23)

The cult of Apollo had an important place in Miletus beginning with the Archaic period until the spread of Christianity. The Delphin (Dolphin), sacred to the cult of Apollo, was known as the protector of seamen and ships. Therefore, in Miletus, with its four harbours, the cult of Apollo Delphinius was very important.

Situated in the vicinity of the Lions' Harbour and dedicated to Apollo Delphinius, the Delphinion was initially built in the Archaic period. The temple, open to the sky, consisted of a large area surrounded on all four sides by walls, with an altar in the centre. Remains from the Archaic period are not sufficient to provide adequate information.

Present day remains belong to the temple built in the Hellenistic and Roman periods.

In the Hellenistic period, the temenos, 50 metres wide and 60 metres long, was surrounded by Doric stoas and the temple could be entered by three doors on the west.

In the Roman period the stoas were built in the Corinthian style and the entrance on the west was made into a monumental gate (propylaeum). In the centre, the remains of the foundations of the 4.01 meter long and 3.43 meter wide altar show characteristics of the Archaic period. Corner acroteria and ornamenlalien on cornice fragments disco-vered, give evidence that the altar was erected in the 6th century BC. Inscriptions on which the names of the persons who conducted the yearly ceremonies appear, have also been dated back to this period. In the central part of the temple besides the altar foundations there are also semi-circular platforms (exedra) a round pedestal and portable altars.

A great number of inscriptions discovered in the temple indicate that the Delphinion was used as the state archives. These inscriptions relate to subjects such as texts of treaties negotiated with other cities, matters relating to the city and inscriptions of dedication.

One other feature of the temple was that the annual festival and celebrations held in the Didymaion, were begun in the Delphinion.

# THE NORTH AGORA

# (Plan-III; 24 a, b, c,)

Extending on a large area from the Bouleuterion to the Harbour Stoa, the North Agora consisted of there sections. Believed to have been first built in the 5th century BC, the agora had in later years undergone many alterations. In the Hellenistic period (3rd and 2nd centuries BC) there was no west stoa. The agora was, entered through a propylaeum on this side and the agora temple stood in the exact centre of the west side. The temple, of a prostyle plan with four Ionic columns in front, shows Hellenistic characteristics. Later, two-storeyed shops were built into the south and south-west stoas. In the last century BC, a propylaeum was built on the east side of the agora giving onto the Sacred Way, however this door was annulled in the 2nd century AD. The row of back shops was built in this period. Some of the shops opened onto the agora, and others onto the Sacred Way. The encircling of the agora on all four sides by stoas was completed in the Roman period. The square-shaped little agora, at the north-west corner of the big agora, was surrounded by stoas with Doric columns. At the rear parts of the stoas were rows of shops. The agora could be entered through passages between the shops. No shops can be seen in the north stoa.

The third section of the North Agora, opening onto the harbour, is the Harbour Stoa. Lying on an east-west axis, the stoa had a northerly extension at right angles to the main building at its west end. To the west of this wing is another section of the North Agora with two doors, one on the north and one on the south, and surrounded by Doric stoas. The length of the Harbour Stoa is approximately 32 metres and contains a row of thirty shops. To the west of the stoa, built in the Doric style, are the harbour monuments. The latrina also stands here. However, as it is mostly destroyed, not many remains can be seen.

*The Harbour Stoa of the north agora and the harbour monument.*

*Harbour monument, 2nd century BC.*

# THE HARBOUR MONUMENTS

## (Plan-III; 25)

There were two harbour monuments in Miletus. Both of these stood in the north-west corner of the Harbour Stoa in front of the Lions' Harbour. The 7.5 meter high greater harbour monument rested on a stepped round lower structure of 11 metres in diameter. On top of the steps stood a high three-cornered base with profiles in the lower part and mouldings in the upper. All there sides of the base were concave, and on top of this base was a section ornamented with reliefs. This part had given the appearance of a ship by making its corners in the form of ships' prows and bows, and the reliefs represented Tritons and Dolphins (Form-22). A prism, with the inscription of dedication on it, stood above the band of reliefs and on top of it all rested a cauldron on a tripod. This couldron, rising over figures of crouched lions, is the piece which was discovered in the Bouleuterion excavations and was then taken to the Museum of Pergamum in East Berlin. The stone workmanship of the structure is characteristic of the 2nd century BC. According to inscriptions changing along with the periods however, the monument is believed to have been dedicated to Ponpeius who was victorious over the pirates in 63 BC and then to Emperor Augustus for his victory in the battle of Actium (31 BC).

The second monument, of smaller dimensons, was a small model of the first one. This 5.36 meter high monument was decorated with Corinthian capitals. The inscription of dedication bears the name of C. Grattio C. F. Gal (eria). Both of these monuments are destroyed and their fragments are in the vicinity.

*Reliefs of Tritons and Dalphins, the harbour monument.*

**FORM 22** *Harbour Monument (Reconstruction)*

*Palastra of the Roman baths and in the background, the Calidarium and Apodyterium.*

# THE ROMAN BATHS

# (Plan-III; 26)

Between Derviş Tekkesi and Pireli Han to the north of the city lie the ruins of large baths, 53 metres long and 28.5 metres wide. The heavily destroyed building had its palaestra and entrance on the south. Styles of two different periods have been recognized in the building. The tepidarium, with columns in the centre and rooms surrounding it, was in the shape of a house with a peristyle. The parts of the building still standing, are the calidarium and the apodyterium.

# THE DEMETER TEMPLE

This temple, revealed in the excavations made in the north-western end of Humeytepe to the north of the city.(Plan-III, M).is 9 metres wide and 20 metres long. The remains of the building indicate that the temple rested on a four-stepped crepis. To the east of the temple are the foundations of the 3 meter wide and 4 meter long altar, and to the south, the temenos walls.

*The church of Micheal and the palace of the head priest, 6th century AD.*

# THE CHURCH OF MICHAEL

The three-winged building located to the west of the North Agora is in the form of a basilica. The church was built over the temple of Dionysius. One can see in front of the apse the remains of the benches on which the priests sat. The columns in the naves have Corinthian capitals. Each nave has six rows of colums. The atrium is at the north of the long side of the church, and the baptistery is at the south-east corner. It is established from an inscription found that the church was built in 600 AD.

The building complex consisting of a large hall to the north of the church, a deep apse with a closed front on the west side and a great number of rooms round it, is accepted to be the palace of the head priest. This large building has been covered to protect the pavement mosaics. It is believed that this building was also built during the same period as the church.

*Heroon, Roman period.*

# THE HEROON

# (Plan-III; 27)

The Heroon situated between the Church of Michael and the Faustina Baths is 46 metres long and 28 metres wide. The building contained a courtyard, a tomb chamber, an altar and rooms on the south side (Form-24). The courtyard was surrounded by columns with Corinthian capitals, and in the centre stood the square-shaped tomb chamber. Understood from the remains to have been covered by a dome, the tomb chamber had two doors, one on the north and the other on the south. Inside the building were niches. Between the two niches on the south side stood the altar, 3.81 metres long and 2.40 metres wide, and on top of it, a sarcophagus ornamented with garlands and Nike reliefs reflecting has characteristics of the Roman Empire period. The large room in the centre of the south side of the courtyard was in the form of a exedra. The other three rooms had doors opening onto the south.

*Altar, the heroon.*

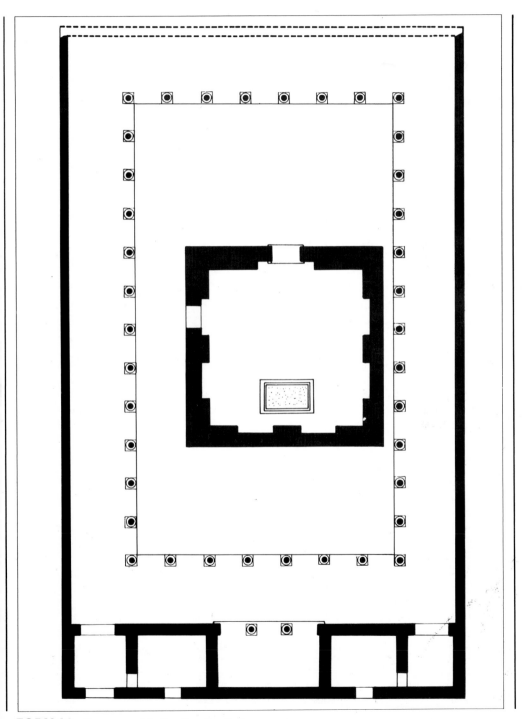

**FORM 24**  *Heroon next to the Faustina Baths*

# THE MOSQUE OF ILYAS BEY ITS COMPLEX BUILDINGS

## (Plan-III; 28)

The Mosque of Ilyas Bey, situated to the south of the South Agora, constitutes a complex with its Medrese and Baths. The mosque built in 1404 by Ilyas Bey, Emir of Menteşe during the period of principalities, and named after him, is one of the most remarkable buildings of miletus. Because it is in quite good condition and displays fine stone workmanship, the mosque has an important place in the history of art.

The mosque has a square plan of 18 metres a side, a single dome and a minaret. The minaret fell down in 1955. The upper parts of the rubble walls are faced with white marble. In certain sections of the building coloured marble was used, thus providing a striking feature to the details of the decoration.

*Entrance facede, the mosque of Ilyas Bey,*

*The mosque of Ilyas Bey and the ensemble of neghbouring buildings, 1404, AD.*

The transition from the square plan to dome is achieved by corner arches and pendants; the dome is made of bricks.

The portal (entrance) is formed by three arched partitions separated by two columns inside a high, deep and pointed niche. Of these partitions, only the middle one was used as a door, the other two were closed with marble grids and turned into windows. The inscription on the upper part of the door panel is encircled by edgings with geometrical and stylized motifs of palmettoes and lotus leaves.

Stalactitic capitals, window sides and grids, all reflect a careful workmanship. The niche for the Imam is a work of art in itself. In the upper part of the niche which is decorated with edgings of stalactitic and various geometrical motifs is an inscription, also decorated with a stalactitic edging. On both sides of the inscription are oil lamps, and in the lower part, two little ornamented niches. The actual niche stands in the centre of all this decoration. The niche, of pyramidal form, has in the middle a band of inscriptions. Not the slightest empty space

*Stone workmanship on the portal of the mosque of Ilyas Bey, detail.*

*Derviş Tekkesi.*

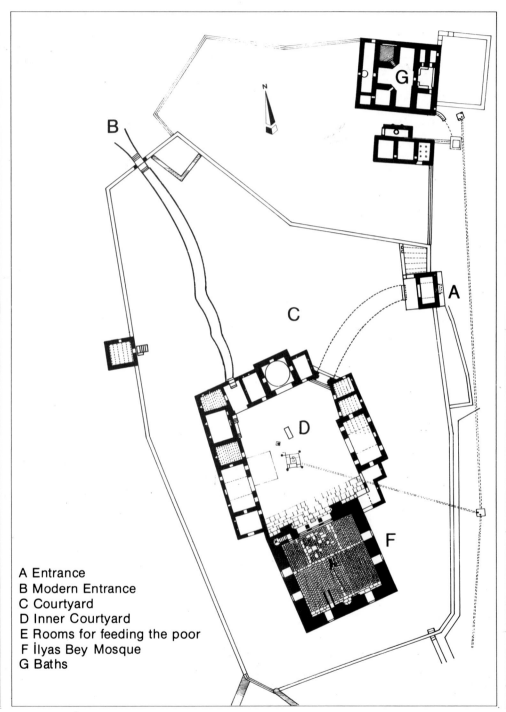

A Entrance
B Modern Entrance
C Courtyard
D Inner Courtyard
E Rooms for feeding the poor
F İlyas Bey Mosque
G Baths

**FORM 25  İlyas Bey Mosque and complex**

has been left in the whole of the niche, and all details have been carefully worked.

The Mosque of Ilyas Bey covers a large area and has two courtyards, a large one outside and a smaller one inside. The inner courtyard is surrounded by the dining rooms of the charity kitchen. In the courtyard a great number of tombs and tombstones with epitaphs can be seen (Form-25).

One sees in Miletus a great number of buildings from the period of the Principality of Menteşe:

The double-domed Derviş Tekkesi, situated to the north of the city is heavily destroyed. To the west of it, the Caravanserai (Pireli Han), about 29 metres long and 24 metres wide, contains a courtyard and rooms for overnight stops. It is understood froom the stairs in the courtyard that the building was two-storeyed.

The building named the "Four-columned Mosque", located to the south of the Heroon on the lower slopes of the theatre hill was built on a simple plan. The niche for the Imam was built of bricks. To the north of the theatre are the remains of a mosque also belonging to the same period.

Another building lying between the Church of Michael and the Heroon is the "Forty-stepped Mosque". The remains to the south-west of this mosque belong to the Menteşe Baths. Still another building is a small mosque standing near the West Gate of the South Agora.

In the museum which was opened in 1973 in Miletus as a local museum, Milesian findings are displayed. The museum contains various works belonging to the Mycenaean, Classical, Archaic, Hellenistic, Roman, Byzantine, Seljuk and Ottoman periods.

The baths facing the museum were built in the Roman period.

*Detail of ornament, niche for the Imam.*

# THE WELL-KNOWN PERSONAGES OF MILETUS

The most important centre of Ionian philosophy was the city of Miletus. Among the eminent philosophers of Miletus one can name Thales, Anaximander, and Anaximenes. Although these philosophers differed greatly from one another in their theses, it is beyond any doubt that they played a very important role in initiating scientific thought and were its precursers.

Thales who was recognized by Aristotle as the first of philosophers was at the same time a mathematician, an astronomer and a physicist. Thales was born in 625 BC in Miletus. Although not much information exists on his life, it is known that he went to Egypt to further his learning, and discovered the theorem known by his name, the Thales Theorem, in geometry. Thales, who had enough knowledge of astronomy to be able to predict the solar eclipse of May 585, was also the founder of the Ionian philosophy of Nature.

Anaximander, a pupil of Thales, claimed the essential substance to be "the unlimited" and "the endless", and to prove the belief that the Earth was in the form of a cylinder in the middle of the ocean. He made a map of the world.

On the other hand, Anaximenes who lived between the years 550 and 480 BC, claimed that the essential substance was air and that all the phenomena in the universe were dependent on air. It is also said that he further developed the sundial invented by Anaximander.

The historian and geographer Hecataeus, used the word "history" for the first time to mean "research", and wrote a book summarizing the history of the Greeks. He also collected his travel notes in a book called "Tour Round the World".

The well-known architect and town planner of the beginning of the 5th century BC, Hippodamus, was also a Milesian. Another architect was Isidorus who lived in the 6th century AD. Isidorus was renowned for building the Church of Saint Sophia in 537 AD.

# DIDYMA

# DIDYMA

The Apollo temple of Didyma (the Didymaion), located within the boundaries of the village of Yeni Hisar in the Söke district of the province of Aydın, was known as a sanctuary and seat of an oracle attached to Miletus. Recent excavations revealed remains which showed that Didyma was not only a seat of an oracle but also the site of dense settlement.

The research concerning the origins of the names of Didyma and Didymaion has been a subject of discussion going on for years. Along with several other myths, it was thought that the name Didymaion which meant "twin temples" or "temple of the twins", was related to Artemis, the twin sister of Apollo. However, as no definite evidence could be found, this theory also remained as a myth. With the intensification of work in recent years on the "Sacred Road" con-

*The remaining standing columns on the south-east corner and view of the pronaos.*

*Front facede, the Didymaion, Hellenistic period.*

117

necting Miletus and Didyma, and the finding of the place of the Artemis cult during the excavations however, it was proved that this thesis was right. The two temples built for the twin brother and sister, the Artemision and the Didymaion, constitute the origin of the name Didyma.

Apollo and Artemis were closely related to the mother goddess Cybele who had, from prehistoric times, a very important place in Anatolia. The mother goddess Cybele had various names (such as Kubaba, Isis, Hepat, Lat) and epithets according to localities and cultures. The most widespread of these names was Dindymene which was derived from mount Dindymus and which is remarkable for its resemblance to the name Didyma.

The name of Apollo is considered not to be Greek. Apollo, who, because of the resemblance in names was identified with the god Apulunas mentioned in Hittite written sources, represented shape given by rational perception, temperate power, fine arts and light. Besides these, he was renowned for his ability to prophesy, and he communicated to people through mediums and oracles his knowledge of the future.

The dependence of communities on religion increased as it was seen that gods possessed forces to direct according to their will, all phenonema and events relating to natura and society. As a natural consequence of the increase in religion, belief in the power to prophesy of the gods who could foresee events and phenonema was intensified.

In the Archaic period the oracle of Apollo had great fame. The great number of temples erected in Anatolia as seats of oracles is evidence that belief in gods had reached enormous proportions. The most important of the temples dedicated to Apollo were the Temple of Apollo at Delphi in Greece, and the Didymaion in Anatolia. These two seats were in constant rivalry with each other. A fine example of this rivalry can be clearly seen in the following verses by the oracle of Delphi.

"And that day, Miletus, on that day,
You, the badly organized city,
You shall be ample prey to the enemy,
A table of festivities to hordes and hordes of people!
Your woman will wash the feet,
Of warriors of long hair and beard,
And foreigners will, Oh Didyma,
Lay hands on your temple".

In the mid 7th century BC, in the oracles of Apollo, the god could be consulted once a year for official matters, and the answers recevied to questions directed would be in the form of "yes or "no". When in later years, consulting the god also for private matters became a tradition, these consultations became gradually more frequent. The oracles of Apollo grew very rich as a result of this, and their fame and influence spread over large areas. They became as powerful as the state they were in and were effective in shaping the destinies of persons and communities, and particularly in politics where they played a very important role, they very often caused wrong decisions to be taken.

Pausanias states that the Apollo temple at Didyma had been built before the Greek colonization (10th century BC). It is believed in the light of this that the existence of Didyma, like that of Miletus and Priene, goes back to the 2nd millennium BC. However according to the results of excavations and research work undertaken up to the present day, the earliest temple remains date back to the end of the 8th century BC.

One learns from Herodotus that valuable votive offerings were presented to the temple by King Necho of Egypt at the end of the 7th century BC, and by King Croesus of Lydia in the 6th century BC.

It is believed that the construction of the

Archaic temple was begun in the mid 6th century BC and was completed at the end of the same century. In the 6th century BC, the Didymaion was administered by a priestly caste named Branchids. During this period which lasted about 100 years, the temple flourished and went through its most brilliant era.

It was completely burned and plundered by the Persians during the battle of Lade, the priests of the temple were driven to Susa, and the cult statue of Apollo was taken to Ecbatana. The statue of Apollo which was dated back to 500 BC, was made by the sculptor Kanachus of Sicyon and reflects Anatolian-Hittite characteristics.

The construction of the Hellenistic temple was begun after the victory of Alexander the Great over the Persians. However, it was understood from the remains that this Hellenistic temple was not completed.

The temple of which the construction was continued under Emperor Caligula (37-41 AD) who wanted to be thought of as the god of the temple, and later under Hadrian (117-138 AD), was never completed. With the alterations made in the 3rd century AD to protect it from plunder, the temple took on the appearance of a fortress, and flourished under the reigns of Aurelian (270-275) and Diocletian (284-305).

There are findings which indicate that work was done on the temple during the reign of Emperor Julian (361-363).

In the beginning of the 5th century AD, Emperor Theodosius had a church built in the sacred courtyard (Adyton-Sekos). This church, which had the appearance of a three-winged basilica, was destroyed in an earthquake and later rebuilt with one wing (9th century AD).

In the 10th century AD, the two-columned hall (Chresmographeion - hall of the oracle) and the pronaos, which were used as storage areas, were greatly damaged in a fire, and most of the marble turned into lime.

After the Seljuks and the Mongols conquered

*General view of the south side of the temple.*

the region the temple was completely abandoned.

An Italian traveller who visited Didyma in 1446 records that the whole temple was standing, however, at the end of the 15th century the temple was completely destroyed by an earthquake and turned into a heap of marble. In later years the temple was used as a quarry, and many of its architectural elements were used as building material in the construction of dwellings and other buildings by the local people.

# EXCAVATIONS

The first excavations in Didyma were made in 1858 by the English under the direction of Newton. The area excavated was the Sacred Road.

In the temple, excavations were first begun in 1872 by the French under O Rayet and A Thomas. The aim was to find the cult statue of Apollo, but at the end of the work which lasted two years, the cult statue had not been found. However, it had been possible to determine the dimensions of the temple and to reconstruct its plan.

In the excavations of 1895-96, again undertaken by the French, the work, supervised by B Haussoullier and E Pontremoli, was concentrated on the northern part of the temple. These excavations were stopped shortly after due to economic reasons. Excavations begun in 1905 for the museums in Berlin under the supervision of Th. Weigand, were continued on a systematic basis until the year 1937. During this time a great portion of the temple was revealed. After this date, excavations were interrupted and work on publication of the results was begun.

In order to find solutions to certain problems concerning the temple and its surroundings, excavations were begun again in 1962, this time for the German Institute of Archaeology, under the supervision of R Naumann. When R Naumann left, the excavations in Didyma were continued under the supervision of Klaus Tuchelt. Work is at present still going on in the area with special attention to research on the Sacred Road.

*Row of columns in pronaos.*

# THE SACRED ROAD

The Delphinion is accepted as the starting point of the Sacred Road connecting Miletus and Didyma. The road ran from the Sacret Gate of Miletus southwards in the direction of the coast to Panarmos Harbour (above Akköy), and bending south-east from the port, reached the Didymaion. Within the boundaries of Yenihisar, the Sacred Road runs close along the side of the asphalt road. A portion of the Sacred Road has been revealed by excavations and exploratory trenches dug in recent years. However, due to certain bureaucratic obstacles, it has not yet been possible to establish its connection to the temple.

On either side of the road there were statues of Branchids (priests and priestesses attached to the temple), crouching lions and sphinxes, all of which gave the road an impressive appearance. Monumental tombs and sarcophagi belonging to important persons were also dispersed along the road. Statues of Branchids revealed in the excavations carried out by Newton in 1858 on the Sacred Road have been taken to the British Museum. Some fragments belonging to the statues are in the storeroom of the house of excavations in Didyma. Four of the Branchid statues in which Hittite influence is apparent and which have been dated back to the 6th century BC, are on display in the museum in Miletus. In the years 100 and 101 AD Emperor Trajan had the Sacred Road restored. The parts of the road that had fallen down were raised to a higher level and the other parts were repaired. Inscriptions indicate that the restoration work was completed in a very short time.

It was understood from a milestone revealed during excavations that the road was 16.5 kilometres long. According to the portions uncovered, the width of the road which was made of stone blocks, changed between 5 and 7 metres. On both sides of it were rows of shops, votive fountains, monumental tombs, baths, and the area for the cult of Artemis. Findings indicate a dense settlement. The group of people who set out from Miletus to join the annual celebrations and festivities which were held in the Didymaion every spring, reached the temple after a long walk, there were therefore, resting places on the Sacred Road. It is understood that the Terrace with the Sphinx, uncovered during excavations carried out in 1985 about 4 kilometres to the south of Akköy, was a halting place built for rest purposes.

*The, Sacred Road connecting Miletus and Didyma, Archaic-100 AD.*

*Ionic capital.*

# THE ARCHAIC DIDYMAION
## The Apollo Temple at Didyma

Remains of foundations of the Late Geometric period were found during excavations carried out in 1962 by German archaeologists within the secos of the Hellenistic temple to look for the first Apollo temple of Didyma which, according to Pausanias, had existed before the 10th century BC. The temple which, according to the foundations of secos walls uncovered in the north and south parts, was 10.20 metres wide and 24 metres long and slightly narrowed towards the east, was built at the end of the 8th century BC. The small and simple temple contained a secos (sacred courtyard), an altar, a sacred source, a cult statue and the symbols of Apollo. The Late Geometric temple did not have a naiscos, the naiscos is understood to have been built at the end of the 7th century BC to protect the cult statue. Exploratory digging carried out to the south-west of the temple revealed the remains of a columned building 15.50 metres long and 3.60 metres wide. The remnants and ceramic findings have been dated back to the end of the 7th century BC. (Form-26, 26a).

Not many remains are left to the present day from the Archaic Didymaion, as it was burned, destroyed and plundered in 494 BC (the battle of Lade). Besides, findings relating to the Archaic temple are further limited by the fact that the Hellenistic temple was built over the foundations of the Archaic one. However, the construction of the plan was possible and various examples of reconstruction were made through ancient authors, as well as architectural and sculptural fragments found during borings and excavations.

The Didymaion became really important in the first half of the 6th century BC when all Ionian cities, and especially Miletus, reached their most flourishing era. The temple was rebuilt in 560-550 BC with larger proportions. The influence of the temples of Hera at Samos and Artemis at Ephesus are apparent in the Archaic Didymaion.

The temple, an 87.65 metre long and 40.89 metre wide building of a dipteral plan (having a double row of columns all around), rested on a two-stepped crepis. The longer sides had 21 columns each, the east had 8, and the west 9, whereas in the pronaos there were 8 columns in two rows. Together with the columns within the peristasis (the surrounding hall), the total number of columns added up to 112.

The parts of the temple which were not visible from the outside were made of local tufa, while those that were visible were made of marble. The marble was provided from marble quarries on the island of Taşoz, and in the hills above the village of Pınarcık near Bafa lake. One can still see fragments of roughly prepared column shafts in the quarries at Pınarcık. The partly worked marble, brought from the quarry to Latmos Harbour, was then taken by sea to Panarmos Harbour, and from there it was carried to the temple.

The bases and capitals of the 15.45 metre high columns bear the characteristics of the Artemis Temple at Ephesus; the bases consist of tori and double trochili, the Ionic capitals have large volutes, the column shafts have 36 flutes. On the eastern facade, the lower parts of the columns in the front row were decorated with reliefs; a head of a woman (Kore) from these reliefs is on display in Charlottenburg Museum in Berlin. The characteristics of all these elements indicate that they were at the latest made in the year 550 BC, which coincides with the date of the initial construction of the Archaic Didymaion.

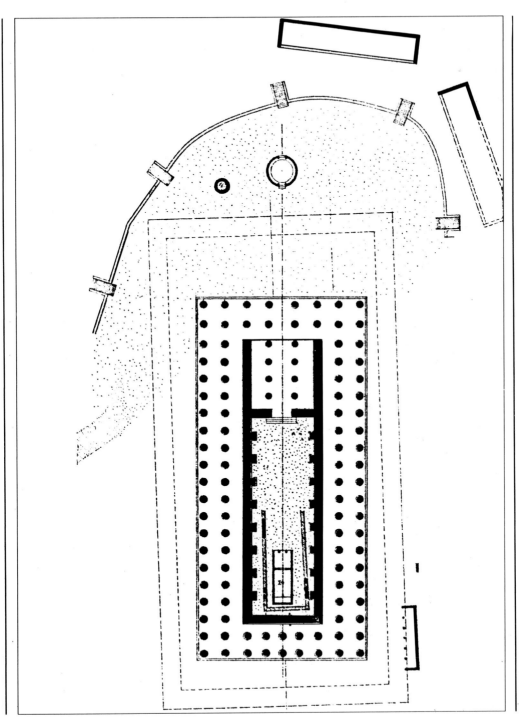

**FORM 26** *Archaic Didymaion*

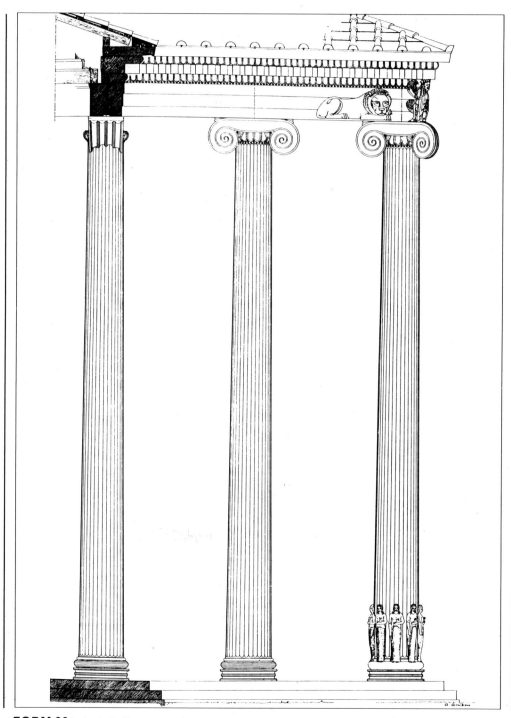

**FORM 26a** *Archaic Reconstruction*

The double row of columns in the pronaos indicate that it had a roof. The architrave is quite narrow. In the corners are highreliefs of winged gorgons and behind these are figures of crouching lions. It is believed that certain wild animals' figures were also there besides the lions. This type of decoration is quite unusual in temple entablature. These pieces of work which can be dated back to the end of the 6th century BC, were probably made during restoration works which took place in the temple at the time. On the architrave rest, in due order, a band of egg-and-dart moulding, dentils, another band of egg-and-dart moulding, a cornice and a roof.

The inner sides of the walls of the secos (sacred courtyard) were fortified by pilasters in the form of half-columns, which brought colour to the long, high walls. The height of the walls of the 50.25 metre long and 17.45 metre wide secos reached 17.5 metres. Walls of this height give the impresion that the secos was roofed, but the greatness of the distances between the pilasters on the walls destroys this theory.

Within the secos stood the naiscos (little temple) where the cult statue of Apollo was kept. However, there are not many findings belonging to this building. During borings in the Hellenistic naiscos, foundation remains belonging to a smaller building were found. It is believed that these foundations belong to the Archaic naiscos. The bronze cult statue is known as the "Apollo Philesius" and represents Apollo catching a deer.

In front of the temple (east) and on the same axis stands a circular altar. This altar, of which the outer diameter measures 8 metres and the inner one 5.5 metres, had two doors. The holes for the hinges can still be seen on the thresholds. The altar of which the inside is very well preserved, had been used in the Archaic, and also in the Hellenistic and Roman temples as the sacred place where

Detail of column bases, sea creature.

the animals presented as votive offerings were burned. The great amount of ashes found in the building during excavations is evidence of this. In ancient times, animals offered to the gods of the sky were burned in this type of altar, and sanctification was achieved by washing in the blood of the animals offered to the gods under the ground. To the north of the altar is the sacred source. The masonry of the lower parts of this circular well shows that it was constructed in the Archaic period.

3.5 metre high protective walls encircle the front part of the temple. These walls must have been built to diminish the difference of levels in the large area in front of the temple. In the uncovered portion of these protective walls were five outlets with staircases, each 2.5 metres wide. The central stairs are situated just opposite the altar, on the same axis. These stairs led to the terrace on which stood the votive and gods' statues. The style of the egg-and-dart moulding used to decorate the upper part of the terrace wall as well as the workmanship of the wall and stairs, bear the characteristics of the Archaic period.

On this terrace one also comes across the remains of two long structures built of limestone. The 34.5 metre long and 7 metre wide buildings must have been shops where visitors took shelter or shopped. These buildings also show the characteristics of the Archaic period.

Next to the stairs along the terrace wall situated in the direction of the south-east end of the temple are rows of benches. It is understood that these benches extending parallel to the steps of the temple were built in the Hellenistic period, and were the rows of benches for the stadium situated to the south of the temple. Every four years festivities called the "Megala Didymeia" and musical shows, were held here, and torch processions and competitions were arr-

*Detail of column base*

anged. The bases having a hole in the centre, which marked the starting points of the races, can be seen at the eastern end of the stadium. These bases lie on the same axis as the altar.

# THE HELLENISTIC DIDYMAION

What remains of the temple in the present day, through hundreds of years of earthquakes, fire, destruction and plunder are mostly remnants of the Hellenistic period (Form-27). The Roman characteristics witnessed in certain parts of the temple, are elements which have reached the present day from the temple, which continued to be built during the Roman period also.

It is known that the construction of the Hellenistic temple was begun in 313 BC, and that it was erected over the Archaic temple which was burned and destroyed in 494 BC. The donations of Alexander the Great and of King Seleucus I of Syria were of great help in the rebuilding of the Didymaion. Furthermore, Seleucus I had the cult statue of Apollo brought back from Ecbatana (300 BC) and replaced in the temple.

The plan of the temple was made by Paionius of Ephesus and Daphnis of Miletus. These two renowned architects had also worked on the Artemision at Ephesus (one of the seven wonders of the world) and the Heraion at Samos, which were considered to be the largest and the most magnificent temples of the Hellenistic period. The Didymaion emerges as the third largest edifice of the Hellenistic period, following the former.

*Head of Gorgon, fragment of frieze, 2nd century AD.*

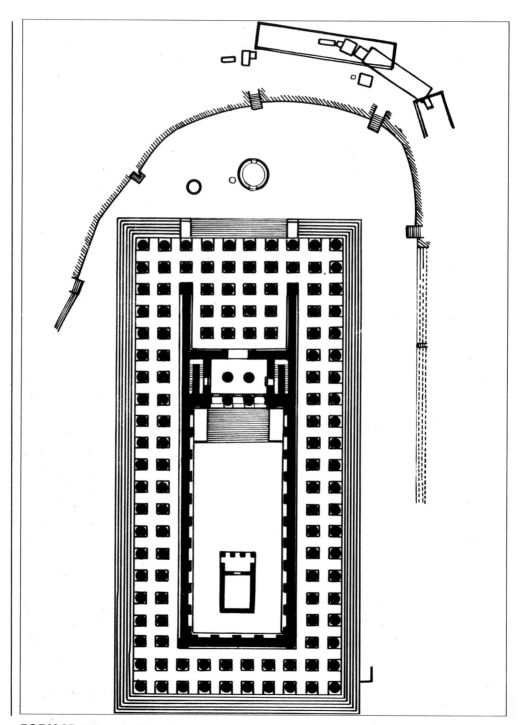

**FORM 27** *Hellenistic Didymaion*

The plan, as a requisition of the cult, had to provide an open air space to hold the Sacred Fountain, the Altar, the Laurel Grove, considered to be the sacred tree of Apollo, and it had also to shelter the cult statue. All these elements had to be arranged in a way not to disturb the covered spaces. The architects constructed an ostentatious example of architecture, by the perfect use of the local characteristics of the cult of the oracle and of the spaces of different levels. This temple differed from a normal temple plan in that it was also the seat of an oracle. The edifice consisted of a long pronaos, a rectangular hall with two columns in the centre (the oracle hall- Cresmographeion), a sacred courtyard surrounded by high walls (Secos - Adyton), and in this courtyard a small temple sheltering the cult statue of Apollo (the naiscos), all set on the same axis but at different floor levels.

The temples, situated over the Archaic one and of Larger proportions, had necessitated an uncommonly high lower structure. The temple rested on a 3.5 meter high and 7-stepped platform (crepis), and had in the centre of the front facade a 14-stepped stairway of which both sides were limited. The width of these stairs was equal to that of the temple. This characteristic is also visible in the Classical Artemision. The temple, 109.34 metres long and 51.13 metres wide, was built on a dipteral (having a double row of columns all around) plan. It had 21 columns each on its longer sides, and 10 each on the shorter ones. Together with the columns within the peristasis and the ones in the pronaos and cresmographeion, the total number of columns added up to 122. The cost of the columns of which only three stand today, was very high. Excavations have revealed a great number of inscriptions showing the calculation of construction costs prepared during the building of the

*The Adyton (Secos) seen from the west.*

temple. It is understood from these documents that the cost of one column was 40,000 drachmae and that the daily wages of a labourer was only 2 drachmae. This means that one labourer would have to work for 20,000 workdays to put a column in its place, or to adapt it to the present day, by assuming that the minimum daily wage of a stone workman be 10,000 TL, the construction cost of a column could be calculated to amount to 200 million TL. It is also known, from these inscriptions that, from 250 BC onwards, 8 archhitects and 20 construction companies worked for the temple.

Such a large and costly building could certainly not have been finished in a short time. It is understood that the construction went on in the 3rd and 2nd centuries BC, and that some of it was completed during the Roman period. Although a great portion of the columns were prepared and set in their places, it can be seen that those in the outer row of the peristasis and especially those in the rear facade were never completed.

*Entrance door of the Cresmographeion and the threshold ornamented with reliefs.*

*The Cresmographeion (the oracle hall), in the backgound the pronaos.*

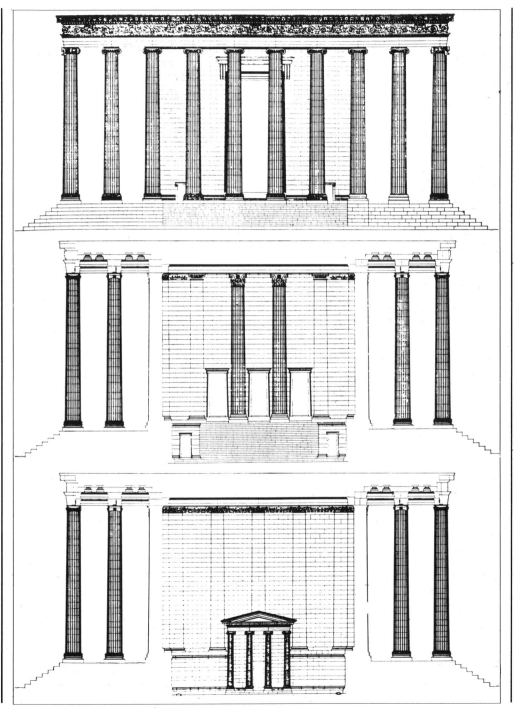

**FORM 28** *Hellenistic Didymaion Reconstruction*

The height of the columns was first determined in 1873 by A. Thomas as being 19.71 metres. The accuracy of the measurement was evidenced by recent research work also. The lower diameters of the columns vary between 1.96 and 2 metres. This conforms to the rule that, in the Ionic order lower diameters of columns are equal to 1/10th of their height (Form 28).

A. von Gerkan has calculated the total height of the temple, including the 19.71 meter high columns, the stepped lower structure and the entablature, as 29.40 metres. This measurement gives an idea of the magnificence of the temple before it was destroyed.

The double row of columns round the temple gave the building a very impressive appearance as well as depth. Of the 108 columns in the peristasis (the peripheral hall) about 80 are standing in their original places. The letters seen in the upper and lower parts of the fragments of column shafts were written by the workmen to avoid any mistakes during the placing of the columns

*Passage (vaulted corridor) to Adyton (the sacred courtyard).*

*Columns fallen in earthquake on the west facede of the temple.*

in their places. This is also an indication that the columns had entasis (a swelling of column shafts).

Of the three Hellenistic coluns still standing, the workmanship of two are complete and they carry the entablature. The third column which carries a capital has no fluting in its shaft. According to the characteristics of the capitals, the columns were built in the first half of the 2nd century BC.

The bases of tne coluns in the peristasis display different characteristics; whereas some consist of plinthus, torus and double trochilus, the column bases in the central part of the outer row in the front facade show Early Roman characteristics. One of these bases is divided in to 12 restangular panels decorated with motifs of sea creatures, palmettoes and other plants. On another base there are double meander and palmento motifs. These bases were built between the years 37 and 41 BC by Emperor Caligula who wanted to identify himself with Apollo.

The capitals situated at the outer corners of the peristasis and ornamented with busts of gods and bulls' heads as well as the heads of Gorgons on the architrave, show the baroque characteristics of the 2nd century AD

The columns on the north side of the temple, of which the workmanship is complete, are all standing in their places, whereas those on the west side were set in their places, although their workmanship was incomplete, the latter now lie on the ground, fallen in earthquakes. Most of the columns on the south side are missing, and it is understood that they were never completed.

In the front of the temple, after the double row of columns, was the pronaos. Also mentioned as the 12-columned hall in archaeological literature, the pronaos had a total of 12 columns in three rows of four columns each, which carried the roof (Dodecastylos). The marks left by the fire of the Middle Ages can be seen on the Attic style, scale motifs are carved on the upper parts of the antae walls are profiled in the same form. This is the first time that this characteristic, of which an example is in the Porthenon, is seen in a Ionic temple.

There were three doors in the rear wall of the pronaos. The central door of monumental appearance was 5.63 metres wide and 14 metres high. The fact that its threshold was placed 1.46 metres higher than the floor of the pronaos shows that there was no entrance from here to the oracle hall. The prophecies of Apollo were communicated by his pronouncers to the people through this door. It is therefore named the "Oracle Door". The marble blocks on either side of the door weigh 70 tons each are known as the heaviest elements of antiquity.

The two other doors, one on either side of the monumental door, were each 1.20 metres wide and 2.25 metres high, and provided the entrance to the inner part of the temple. These doors were connected to the sacred courtyard by vaulted and sloping narrow corridors. In the lower parts of the corridors which opened onto the Adytum were small divisions which had coffering in their ceilings. Doric elements seen on the doors are characteristics which remind one of the propylaea of the Athenian Acropolis. Only persons working in the temple and priests could enter the inner part of the temple. These people would reach the Adytum through the dark and mystic corridors mentioned above.

To the east of the Adytum, between the doors at the end of the corridors, was a 15.24 meter wide stairway consisting of 24 steps. These stairs led to a 14.01 meter long, 8.74 meter wide and 20 meter high hall with three doors and two columns. This hall which had no entrance from the pronaos was the Cresmographeion (the hall of the oracle) which together with the pronaos were the first completed sections of the

*Meander motifs in the ceiling of the Labyrinth.*

temple. Only priests and mediums could enter this hall, and they communicated the prophecies to the people through the above mentioned monumental door. Therefore, the Cresmographeion and the pronaos, which constituted an entity, were considered the most important divisions of the Didymaion. The two columns in the centre of the oracle hall had Corinthian capitals and carried the roof. Understood to have been built in the beginning of the 3rd century BC on the evidence of their characteristics, these capitals are considered to be among the earliest examples of Corinthian capitals.

The doors on the north and south sides of the Cresmographeion open onto stepped passages mentioned as Labyrinths in inscriptions. On the ceiling of the better preserved southern corridor meander motifs can be seen. These passages played an important role in accoustics during cult ceremonies accompanied by the chorus. The roof of the temple was also reached by these passages

The 21.71 meter wide and 53.63 meter long Adytum is of a very striking appearance with its 25 meter high walls and its top open to the sky. The lower part of the Adytum walls which are at the same level as the Cresmographeion have the appearance of a high podium. Their base is profiled and the upper end is finished with a row of egg-and-dart moulding. The podium which is made of smooth marble blocks displays a fine workmanship. In the central parts of the walls are pilasters in the form of half-columns. Over the pilasters were pilaster capitals ornamented with motifs of griffins or voluted plants, on the friezes between the capitals were reliefs representing winged lions holding Apollo's lyre between their paws, and on top of it all was the cornice ending in the cymatium. All these elements brought colour to the long and excessively high walls. The decorations on the walls of the Adytum bear the characteristics of the Early Hellenistic period. These elements indicate that the Adytum was built in the first half of the 2nd century BC. It has also been proven by an inscription that the Adytum had been completed at that time.

One of the most important findings of recent years in the Didymaion are the drawings on the lower parts of the walls of the Adytum. These drawings which can be seen with great difficulty and only under certain lighting condition, first attracted attention in 1979 and work was begun on them in 1980. The work is being carried out by Lother Haselberg who was the first to see the drawings. These were worked onto the smooth marble walls of the Adytum by making about half a millimeter deep incisions in the surface of the marble by a very thin and sharp point, and they represented the plants of various elements and divisions of the Didymaion. In order to obtain accurate drawings, a grid consisting of horizontal lines with 1.8-1.9 centimeter intervals cut at regular intervals by perpendicular lines, was prepared beforehand to serve as a scale. This grid facilitated the making of the actual dravings. It is understood that these drawings which are extremely accurate, were done by the architects who worked on the construction of the temple.

The plans cover an area of 200 square metres. Some of the drawings were made horizontally, whereas others are perpendicular. In general, the horizontal drawings are on a 1 to 1 scale, and the perpendicular ones on a 1 to 6 scale.

Besides the drawings of elements like column bases and shafts, the drawing of a portion of the entablature of the naiscos was also discovered on the rear wall of the Adytum. These drawings, believed to involve all the parts of the temple, will throw a light upon many an unsolved problem on the Didymaion, thus adding new proportions to the work.

To the west of the Adytum stood the naiscos which sheltered the cult statue. The temple, of which only the remains of the foundations can be seen today was 14.43 metres long and 8.24 metres wide. The plan of the naiscos, reconstructed from discovered fragments, was a prostyle. The temple was a small building with antae obtained by the projection of the two side walls of the naos and four Ionic colomns in front. Column bases were of the Ephesus type. The Ionic capitals, antae capitals and entablature ornaments, all show Early Hellenistic characteristics. Wall bases were profiled in the Attic style like the Adytum walls. The edifice, which looked like the Zeus temple at Priene, was the first Anatolian temple built in the Hellenistic period under Attic influence. In contrast with the smooth, ornamentless walls, the entablature was very richly decorated. The coffering of the ceiling in the front hall and the soffits of the lower part of the architrave, were decorated with flower motifs polychromed in various colours. It is accepted, according to the ornamentation of the entablature, that the naiscos was completed in 270 BC and that the cult statue of Apollo which was brought from Ecbatana, was put in its place in the naos in 300 BC.

The reconstruction model of the naiscos, constructed by putting together the discovered architectural fragments, is kept in the storeroom of the excavation house.

*Walls of the Adyton with drawings of plans of the temple.*

# GENERAL CHARACTERISTICS OF THE TEMPLE

Besides being for centuries a very important oracle seat, the Didymaion was als renowned for its sacred water, sacred grove, the many sacred elements it housed, and its wealth. The riches of the temple had its source in donations and votive offerings made in varying forms. The very valuable offerings of King Necho of Egypt, King Croesus of Lydia and King Seleucus II of Pergamum, had an important place among the donations made to the Didymaion. The donation of various sacrifical animals, 1,000 in number, and 12 rams by Lysimachus, was also one of the interesting offerings.

The fact that Miletus attempted to build a fleet with the treasury of the temple before the battle of Lade, shows how rich the Didymaion was.

One other feature of the Didymaion was that it had the right to shelter. This right which was termed "the Right of Asylum", was the recognition of the right of inviolability to people who took refuge in the temple. The right of asylum, which therefore created many problems, had given rise to many a discussion. The boundaries of the right of asylum, however, were gradually enlarged and were increased to 3 kilometres by Emperor Augustus of Rome (44 BC). In later years, Emperor Trajan enlarged the boundaries even more and wanted them to be recognized from the beginning of the Sacred Road.

It is understood from inscriptions that the festivities and ceremonies held every year in spring went on even after the Didymaion was comletely destroyed in 494 BC. The journey from Miletus to the Didymaion was made by sea or by the Sacred Road. The group of people who set out from Miletus with ceremonies begun in the Delphinion where they received the sanctification of Apollo and were sent forward by the Delphins, came

*Example of pilaster capitals in the entablature of the walls of the Adtyon. Reliefs of griffons.*

*General view of the Adyton. In the foreground foundations of the Naiscos (seen from the west).*

*Pilaster capital.*

from the Lions' Harbour to the Panarmos Harbour, and from there reached the Didymaion on foot. First, sacrificial beasts and votive offerings were presented to the god, then, after ceremonies to the accompaniment of music and chorus, the important persons entered the temple, and after that, the questions asked by inquires were answered by the oracle. The ceremonies were directed by the Stephanephors. It was shown by inscriptions that the Emperors Augustus and Trajan took the title of Stephanephor and carried out this position. In the Roman period, the Sacred Road gained in importance as the harbours filled up with alluvial mud and travel by sea became unfeasible.

The reason for this extremely impressive and magnificent temple's not being considered among the seven wonders of the world is related by the authorities to its not having been completed.

# BİBLİOGRAGPHY

**AKURGAL E.**, Ancient Civilization and Ruins of Turkey, İst. 1978.
**BARAN M.**, Milet Kılavuzu, MEB. Ankara, 1965
**BOYSAL Y.**, New Excavations in Caria, Anatolia XI, 1967 s. 32-56
**DEMİRCİOĞLU H.**, Roma Tarihi, Ankara 1953
**DINSMOOR W.B.**, The Architecture of Ancient Greece, London 1950
**DRERUP G., NAUMANN R., TUCHELT K.**, Bericht über die Ausgrabungen in Didyma 1962. AA. 79, 1964, 333-368
**DUYURAN R.**, Priene Kılavuzu, MEB. İstanbul 1948
**ERHAT A.**, Mitoloji Sözlüğü, İstanbul 1984
**GERKAN VON A.**, Das Theater von Priene, München 1921.
**GERKAN VON A.**, Der Naiskos im Tempel von Didyma, Jdl 57, 1942, 183
**GRUBEN G.**, Das archaische Didymaion, Jdl, 78, 1963, s. 78-182
**GRUBEN G.**, Die Tempel der Griechen, München 1976
**HAHLAND W.**, Didyma im 5. Jahrhundert v. Chr. Jdl, 79, 1964, s. 142
**HASELBERGER L.**, Bericht über die Arbeit am Jüngeren Apollontempel von Didyma. İst. Mitt. 1983 (33), S. 90-123
**HERODOT TARİHİ.**, M. Ökmen. A. Erhat, İstanbul 1983
**KINAL F.**, Eski Anadolu Tarihi, Ankara 1962
**KLEINER G.**, Die Ruinen von Milet, Berlin 1968
**MANSEL A.M.**, Ege ve Yunan Tarih, TTK, Ankara 1971
**MALWİTZ A.**, Gestalt und geschichte des jüngeren Athenatem pels von Milet, Jdl, 25, 1975, S. 67
**MALWİTZ A.**, Athena Tempel, İst. Mitt. 18, 1968, 89-143
**MÜLLER-WİENER W.**, Milet 1982
**NUAMANN R., TUCHELT K.**, Ausgrabungen im Südwesten des Tempels von Didyma. İst. Mitt. 13/14, 1963/64, S. 15-62
**ŞENEL A.**, Siyasal Düşünceler Tarihi, Ankara 1982
**SCHEDE M.**, Die Ruinen von Priene, Walter de gruyter com. Berlin 1964.
**SCHEDE M.**, Die Ruinen von Priene, Berlin 1934.
**SCHIERING W.**, Die Minoisch-Mykenische Siedlung in Milet. Jdl, 25, 1975 S. 9.
**THUKYDIDES.**, H. Demircioğlu, I, II. Ankara 1950, 1958.
**TUCHELT K.**, Buleuteriou und Ara Augusti, Jdl, 25, 1975, S. 90.
**TUCHELT K.**, Didyma, İst. Mitt. 23/24, 1973/74
**TUCHELT K.**, Vorarbeiten zu einer Topographie von Didyma. İst. Mitt. Beiheft 9, 1973
**ÜNSAL B.**, Mimari Tarihi, İstanbul 1973
**VOIGTLANDER W.**, Der Jüngste Apollontempel von Didyma, İst. Mitt. Beiheft 14, 1975
**WIEGAND Th., KNACKFUSS H.**, Didyma I, Berlin 1941
**WIEGAND Th., SCHRADER H.**, Priene, Berlin 1904